Writings of My Heart and Soul

Writings of My Heart and Soul

The Fruit of Loving and Praying

"He pierced through my darkness."

BERNICE DUMITRU

XULON PRESS

Xulon Press
555 Winderley Pl, Suite 225
Maitland, FL 32751
407.339.4217
www.xulonpress.com

Paperback ISBN-13: 978-1-66289-081-9
Ebook ISBN-13: 978-1-66289-082-6

THIS BOOK IS DEDICATED

To the Divine Will,
Source of all Goodness and Love!

In memory of my parents,
Ignatius and Pearl Pillart,
who with my three brothers and three sisters,
first showed me Love.

To the Sisters of the Holy Family of Nazareth,
where I learned the ways of God's Love.

In memory of my beloved husband, Teofan,
loving him became my way of holiness.

To all, whose love and friendship,
deepened my understanding of Love.

ACKNOWLEDGEMENTS

My warmest thanks to author, Mike Aquilina, for his kind
endorsement and to Amy Bartoli, Kathy Cleaver,
my niece, Pattie Dentel, and Terri Sullivan
for reviewing my manuscript and making helpful suggestions.
I am most grateful to Carlos Lugo for the photos he took at the
Abbey of Gethsemani, St. Bernard Church, and Puerto Rico,
Mitchell Poljak who took the photos in Death Valley, CA,
Rebecca Covil who drew the Image of the Sacred Heart
and Kris Praskovich who reviewed my photos.
Finally, to all who encouraged me,
cheered me on in this endeavor,
and prayed for me, especially, Sylvia Burleigh
from Xulon Press,
you have my deepest appreciation.

EPIGRAPH

When I was fifteen years old,
a problem was deeply troubling my family.
Feeling the tension, I prayed about it.
That night I had a dream!
I walked out of our home into the back yard.
There Jesus was sitting, smiling, and waiting for me.
He reached out His Hand and took mine in His and said,
"Don't worry."
I carry that dream in my heart.
The little poem on the next page that I discovered
about the same time,
expresses my life's guiding principle.

Bernice Dumitru

Divine Providence

You know the way for me,
You know the time,
Into your Hands,
I trustingly place mine.
Your plan is perfect,
Born of Perfect Love,
You know the way for me,
That is enough.

-anonymous

Table of Contents

INTRODUCTION

"*Where do we begin? Begin with the heart.*" This quote from Juliana of Norwich spoke to me as I thought about this introduction. As I worked on the book, it was like a living thing, growing while I was trying to finish it. My poems were still alive with the feelings I had experienced while writing them. I even found myself tweaking them as I experienced grace anew in my heart.

I have been writing poetry since I was fourteen. The spark was Sister Beatrice, my first-year English teacher. She encouraged us to author a poem for the National Anthology of Poetry. I composed two that were chosen for publication, "The Woman," included in this book and, "The Sudden Night," which I sadly lost. But I remember the theme that inspired that poem, it was the 'sudden night' that came on at the Crucifixion of Jesus. The writing of poems became a part of my response to a growing relationship with God. I experienced God's love early in life, and it was natural that at sixteen, I committed my life to God and became a novice with the Sisters of the Holy Family of Nazareth.

I continued to write, not every day, but whenever a poem would well up within me, sparked by an inner experience, a word of Scripture or an event. My poems began to mark the assorted colors of my inner life and became an outlet for both negative and positive emotions. They came to express my experience of God and my wrestling with both human and divine love in my life.

When I left the religious community at age 43 and married 2 years later, I discovered my husband also wrote poetry, but soon his passion in his retirement became painting. Often, he would say to me, "Why don't you come and paint with me?" My response was "You paint with acrylics, and I paint with words." I love to play with words and images and that comes through in my poems. See "Destination" and "Friendship Verses" in Chapter Five.

Over the years I shared my poems with others who appreciated them. A former spiritual director, Father James Garvey, loved poetry, wrote it himself and would always encourage me to publish my poems. I entered contests but never won. Eventually, my poem, "Three Wishes," was published in a Christmas Issue of *The Sunday Visitor,* and later four others were published by *Catholic 365*, an internet magazine. When Fr. Garvey was diagnosed with cancer in May of 2022, that gave me the impetus to finally take the plunge. An online offer from Xulon Press in September of 2022 was the final push I needed. I was glad I could share with Fr. Garvey, before he died in January of 2023, that I was composing a book of my poems for publication. His final advice," Be sure you have several people proofread it before it is published." As I began seriously working on my manuscript, I heard a message that confirmed my decision. A priest was speaking about grace and remarked that the natural talents we have been given are Graces from God and are meant to be shared.

As I started arranging my poems, I felt more was needed to communicate my experiences. I viewed my poems as fruit produced by the beautiful tree of spirituality. As there was much that nourished my heart to bear this fruit, I decided to include quotes from Sacred Scripture, other authors and saints that spoke to me. These can be found in the text, the Appendices and bibliography. From a simple book of poems, it has become a book of meditations. As I said at the beginning of this introduction, it became a living thing, growing as I tried to finish it. I trust that God's Divine Providence helped me include the poems and excerpts most beneficial for you, my readers.

The writings are arranged in seven chapters. Chapter One is titled, "Love's Overtures." It is God Who always first loves us by making overtures to every soul throughout his/her life. We need to be open to receiving them and realizing God's personal Love for us. That is the beginning of any spiritual life. It is the first grace St. Ignatius invites us to pray for before we move on in the retreat of the Ignatian Spiritual Exercises.

Chapter Two, "Love's Descent," touches on the most extraordinary event that occurred for humanity, God's revelation of Himself in the Incarnation. His own Son came to share our human life, show us the loving Face of the Father, and to die for our salvation. We cannot contemplate enough the Love that came to us in Jesus. St. Teresa of Avila said that in prayer we should always keep before us the Sacred Humanity of Jesus.

In Chapter Three, "Creation Speaks," we see that God's revelation began with Creation. He made it for us and through it shares His Divine Attributes with us. Every person, creature, circumstance and event is an "I love you!" from God. Discovering the trace of the Divine and giving thanks, even in difficult circumstances is a fundamental spiritual practice.

"Sacramental Love," the topic of Chapter Four, is a continuation of "Love's Descent." Through the rituals of the Church, our worship and the Sacraments, Jesus descends even more deeply into our hearts. Through our water, our bread and wine, our vocations, our oil, our sickness, and death, He manifests and shares His Saving Presence and actions within and among us. In this continuing Incarnation He keeps His promise to be with us until the end of time.

Chapter Five looks at "Devotional Love" which is our response to God's overtures, to His outpouring of Love. It is our "I love You" to God said in a myriad of ways. It is the Holy Spirit that makes possible our response. Without Him we can do nothing. Our very desire to pray is His Gift.

"Human Love" taken up in Chapter Six, explores how loving others opens us to receive Divine Love. The more vulnerable we are in loving others the more vulnerable we become before the Divine Lover. Experiencing both the joy and the pain of loving, we begin to understand the magnitude and depth of

God's Love for us. Even when we reject His overtures or do not respond, He loves us freely and eternally.

Finally, Chapter Seven, "Love's Dark Night," addresses our surrender to God's Will in the difficulties of life. Human love needs to be purified and transformed. Because of Adam's sin, we experience a darkness of intellect, a weakness of will and unruly passions. Although Jesus has redeemed us, a healing purification and a reordering takes place usually through both physical and spiritual suffering. Surrender to God's Will even in the most difficult situations, brings peace. Father Dolindo Ruotolo instructs us in the "Surrender Novena" to say daily ten times:

"O Jesus, I surrender to You, take care of everything."

Not having any children of my own, I am happy to have finally given birth to this "literary child." In these writings from my heart and soul I recognize myself but more importantly I confess the Love of God that generated this book. I hope you will find inspiration to find the trace of the Divine in your own life and realize the deep personal Love God has for you. God bless you.

CHAPTER ONE

Love's Overtures

*"...**the love of God has been poured into our hearts through the Holy Spirit that has been given to us.**
At the appointed time, while we were still helpless,
Christ died for the ungodly.
Indeed, it is seldom that anyone will die for a just person,
although for a good person
someone might be willing to die.
Thus, God proved his love for us in that while we were
still sinners Christ died for us.
And so, now that we have been justified by Christ's blood,
how much more certainly will we be saved
through him from divine retribution."*
Romans 5:1-9

"He showed me a little thing the size of a hazelnut,
lying in the palm of my hand,
and to my understanding it was as round as a ball.
I looked at it and thought, 'what may this be?'
and I was answered generally thus,
'It is all that is made.'
I marveled at how it might last,
for I thought it might suddenly fall into nothing for its littleness
and I was answered in my understanding,
'It lasts and ever shall, for God loves it'."[1]

---

[1] Norwich, Juliana. *Revelations of Divine Love.* Chapter 5. New York: Image. 1977.

"Listen to me, O house of Jacob, all who remain
of the house of Israel,
you who have been carried by me since your birth
and borne by me from the womb.
Even when you reach old age, I will still be the same.
Even when your hair is gray, I will still carry you.
I have made you and I will uphold you;
I will carry you and save you."
Isaiah 46:3-4

WAITING LOVE

I have played,
In the garden of my Father's House,
Ever since I was very young.

I have seen Him,
So often, at the window,
Gazing on me with great love.

He waits, while,
I chase after butterflies,
Hoping to catch a beautiful one.

His heart aches,
When I stumble and cry out,
"Why can't I make them mine?"

He will wait there,
Until I tire of my playing,
And run into His loving, welcoming arms.

"Late have I loved you, O Beauty ever ancient,
ever new, late have I loved you!
You were within me, but I was outside,
and it was there that I searched for you.
In my unloveliness I plunged into the lovely things
which you created.
You were with me, but I was not with you.
Created things kept me from you;
yet if they had not been in you,
they would not have been at all.
You called, you shouted, and you broke through my deafness.
You flashed, you shone, and you dispelled my blindness.
You breathed your fragrance on me;
I drew in breath and now I pant for you.
I have tasted you, now I hunger and thirst for more.
You touched me, and I burned for your peace."[2]*

St. Augustine of Hippo. *Confessions.* New York: Image. 1960.

LOVE'S MEETING

Searching,
Seeking,
Longing,
Reaching,
Inner spirit,
Ever stretching,
Heart is yearning,
For Love's touching.

Peace, my soul,
Listen closely.
Silent wings of Love
Enfold thee.
In your seeking
He has found thee,
With your longing
He has bound thee,
Your heart's needing,
His Heart's seeking.

I DELIGHT YOU

Can it be true,
That I delight You?
You, who command the seas,
And bring princes to their knees,
You, who flung the stars in the sky,
And watch over all things from on high,
You, I delight?

You, I delight?
God of tenderness and might,
You, Who knits the baby in its mother's womb,
And writes your children's names,
On Your hand,
You stoop, to rejoice over me,
As a mother rejoices
In her child's gift of a dandelion.

You, I delight?
I delight You, O God!
You, I delight!
In You,
I delight!

"...rejoicing in his inhabited world and delighting in the children of men. "
Prov. 8:31

MY GOD AND ME

Gentle, laughing, tender God,
Playing on the edge of my awareness.

Strong, passionate, loving God,
Bursting in on my consciousness.

Creative, dynamic, living God,
Erupting in my life's presence.

Silent, captivating, consuming God,
Enfolding me in His Presence.

"Woe to anyone who rises up against his Maker...
Does the clay say to the one who molds it,
'What are you doing? Your work makes no sense.'"
Isaiah 45:9

THE POTTER

Clay taken in hand,
Treaded and softened,
Through time and suffering,
Ready now to yield,
To delicate touch,
To skillful hands.

Gently He molds and shapes,
Cutting away
That which has no use,
Hollowing out
An emptiness,
A vessel for Himself.

"Come, let us return to the LORD;
he has wounded us, but he will heal us;
he has struck us down, but he will bind up our wounds.
After two days he will revive us;
on the third day he will raise us up to live in his presence.
Let us know the LORD; let us strive to know him.
His coming is as sure as the dawn;
he will come to us like a shower,
like the spring rains that water the earth."
Hosea 6:1-3

SHARE

How to tell of God -
Incomprehensible infinity,
How to tell of me -
Unintelligible humanity,
How to tell of Him and me -
Indescribable intimacy!

He has taken hold,
Of weak surrender,
Of my painful wounds,
He is the mender,
He claimed me as His own,
With love so tender.

His love brings peace,
Though life is in confusion,
His Love brings pain,
His death becomes the measure,
His Love brings joy,
His Life my only treasure!

YOU JUST LEFT

Your Presence,
Like a fragrance,
Lingers in our world.
I cannot touch You,
Or put my hand into Your side,
Yet I know,
You were just here,
Just a moment ago,
You just left.

Your fragrance,
Lingers in our world.
And I cling,
To that fragrance.
It fills my senses.
I know Your Presence
Deep in my heart!

In Your absence
I long for You!
When will You come again?

Steps Jesus walked from the Kidron Valley to Caiaphas House

"That we may live no longer for ourselves, but for Him..."[3]

HIS PARTINGS

His Hand parts the curtain
Of my life,
Pushing aside the veils
Of daily interests,
worries, distractions.

As He steps through this parting,
in my mind and heart,
The voices of others fade.
Then my eyes see only Him,
And my ears hear, only,
His Words of Love.

---

[3] *Roman Missal.* "Eucharistic Prayer IV." Washington, D.C.:USCCB. 2010.

DANCING WITH GOD

I want to dance with You, God,
To be held in the warmth of Your Embrace,
To feel the strength of Your encircling Arms,
To gaze into Your Eyes and Face,
And move with You to the music,
Of Your Voice.

Then my anxieties and cares,
My daily responsibilities and hurts,
Will be as dust motes,
Suspended,
In the sunlight
Of Your Glance.

Then my world will slip away
In the rhythm of our dance.
And You will be my world,
my universe.
my Life!
I want to dance with You, God!

"May they all be one. As you, Father, are in me and I in you,
may they also be in us so that the world may believe
that you have sent me..."
John 17:21

ALWAYS ONE

We eat our hunger,
And drink our thirst,
Until an immense hunger
and thirst we become,
Capable of being satisfied,
By You alone,
The Infinite One.

Suddenly,
You come
Into our longing emptiness,
Carved by the yearning of a thousand reaches,
Never touching.
And in Your coming,
Surprisingly, we find,
That the solitude space of each
Is only One!
The seeming ************** distance is filled,
By the wonder of Your Presence.
Your Love,
Becomes the bond,
Forever making us One.

For 'In him we live and move and have our being.'
As even your own poets have said, 'We are all his offspring. "
Acts.17:28

GIFT

Father Gift,
Being,
Flowing out to be
Another,
Meeting
Son Gift,
Ever returning,
To the Other,
Moving Sea of Love,
Spirit Gift.

My being is poured out,
I am overflow,
Ever drawn,
By the Father to return.

I am Another,
I am Gift,
Never being,
Without receiving and giving,
Ever in the need of meeting
The Other,
In a moving Sea of Love.

That is why my heart,
Is forever searching,
Seeking,
To be One,
In Love,
With the Other.

*"Thou hast made us for thyself, O Lord,
and our heart is restless until it finds its rest in thee."* [4]

ENFOLDED

From a distance,
I watch and marvel,
At the Love that flows,
From Father to Son,
And circles back again,
Into His Heart.

The Father speaks:
"My Son, all that I have,
You know is Yours,
It is Your inheritance,
I hold nothing back."

The Son replies:
"Whatever You want,
Father, I will do,
I embrace Your Will,
Your Love, and You."

Their Love, Their Embrace,
Is palpable, a Living Being,
A Holy Spirit.
It flows out like a wave,
From the Heart of God,
Engulfing everything in its path.

---

[4]   St. Augustine of Hippo. *Confessions.* New York: Image. 1960.

They turn and look at me.
And this Marvelous Love,
This Holy Spirit draws me,
Into the Father's waiting, open arms,
Into the Son's loving embrace,
Into His encircling wings,
Enfolding me,
In unending Light,
In unending Life,
In unending Love.

"You created my inmost being.
You knit me together in my mother's womb.
I praise you because I am wonderfully made;
awesome are your works, as I know very well;"
Psalm 139:13,14

WHAT ELSE IS THERE

One day a priest said,
"We are woven,
Of the wondrous pure Love of God."
I never thought of it that way,
But what else is there,
But Love,
Itself?
Now, I touch,
The fabric of my cheek,
In wonder.
Now, my heart
Leaps in adoration,
As I gaze
Into the eyes
Of my husband.
Now, I kneel,
Before the least
Of my brothers and sisters.

"But now this is the word of the LORD,
he who created you, O Jacob, and formed you, O Israel.
Have no fear, for I have redeemed you.
I have called you by name; you are mine."
Isaiah 43:1

MOMENT OF GRACE

It was a moment of Grace!
Kneeling before the Tabernacle,
In silent prayer,
My whole being was held,
In Your wondrous Light.
My mind reeled,
With an incredible awareness,
Of Your Presence.

"You are Mine."
You said to me,
And I was lost,
In the embrace of Your Light!

Now like thunder
Echoing in the hills,
This moment of ecstasy
Echoes in my life.

Again, and again,
I know Your embrace,
As I remember,
This moment of Grace.

Yosemite Valley, CA

Blood of Christ, inebriate me.
Water from the side of Christ, wash me." [5]

THE DWELLING PLACE

I was drawn by an unseen Presence,
To this mysterious cave-like dwelling,
Knowing not what I would find,
Knowing, only this was the place,
The only place for me.

A profound stillness encompassed me.
A brilliance so wondrous, shone,
Not just around, but within me,
Piercing my heart
With shafts of healing light.

A stream of water cleansed and refreshed me,
Awakening me to a depth of life,
I had not known before.
"Who carved this place of beauty,
A dwelling so peaceful, so deep, so healing?"

Suddenly, a Presence welcomed me,
"I have called you by name; you are Mine."[6]
His Words held me and inebriated me,
Like the choicest wine.
I knew then, I would always dwell here,
In the Wound of His Heart. [7]

---

[5] "Anima Christi," 16th century Prayer attributed to St. Ignatius Loyola, recited as a prayer after Holy Communion, see Appendix A.

[6] *Isaiah* 43:1.

[7] See Appendix B for Juliana of Norwich's description of a vision of Jesus looking at us in His Heart.

"Who then can separate us from the love of Christ?
Will hardship, or distress,
or persecution, or famine, or nakedness,
or danger, or the sword? ...
For I am convinced that neither death, nor life,
nor angels, nor principalities,
nor present things, nor things to come,
nor powers, nor height, nor depth,
nor any other creature will be able to separate us,
from the love of God in Christ Jesus our Lord."
Rom. 8:35,38-39

OMEGA

My life's journey,
Was Pierced
By a Radiant Love,
Energizing me
Toward eternity.
My human heart
Was seeking,
Longing to be,
What it was not,
And yet is,
In its very essence.
Empty and open,
Love's force
Takes hold of my nothing,
Bonds of space and time
Are broken.
My Heart is drawn,
Irrevocably,
To the Divine Center,
To dwell ever
In the Heart of God. [8]

---

[8] Omega is the last letter of Greek alphabet and implies here that God is the end toward which we are oriented.

"Before I formed you in the womb I knew you,
and before you were born, I consecrated you.
I appointed you as a prophet to the nations."
Jeremiah 1:5

SAMUEL

God calls his name,
"Samuel."
The unborn stirs
Unconsciously conscious
Of the Lord's call,
Waiting emptiness grows.
Listening gives birth to a man,
With heart open to silence.

God speaks again,
"Samuel."
Response awakens,
In the heart of giving man,
Surrender deepens,
He yearns to abandon all.

In precious moments,
The soundless Voice names him,
"Samuel."
Words spill out the joyful gift,
"Speak Lord,
I love to listen to Your Voice!
See, Lord,
Here I am!" [9]

---

[9] *1 Samuel* 3.

CHAPTER TWO

Love's Descent

*"For God so loved the world that he gave his only Son,
so that everyone who believes in him may not perish
but may attain eternal life."*
John 3:16

"In His Father's Arms"
Painted by my father 80 years ago.

"In the beginning was the Word, and the Word was with God,
and the Word was God.
He was with God in the very beginning.
Through him all things came into existence,
and without him there was nothing.
The true light that enlightens everyone
was coming into the world.
He was in the world, the world had come
into existence through him,
yet the world did not recognize him.
He came to his own, but his own did not accept him.
However, to those who did accept him
and who believed in his name
he granted the power to become children of God,
who were born not from blood or human desire
or human will, but from God.
And the Word became flesh and dwelt among us.
And we saw his glory, the glory as of the Father's only Son,
full of grace and truth."
John 1:1-2, 9-14

THE DOORS! THE DOORS!

An angel with a flashing sword,
Stood watch before the closing doors,
"You cannot go again within.
This Paradise is closed by sin!"

But God is always 'open door.'
"This, I will tolerate, no more!
I promise you, that One will come,
He will open all and make Us One."

The blood is splashed above the door.
An angel passes with a sword.
"We're saved behind these blood-marked doors!"
God's Chosen people praise their Lord!

Before an open door, amazed,
An angel speaks, "Hail, Full of Grace!"
God's Spirit enters Mary's space,
Her womb will fashion God's own Face!

Elizabeth stands at open door,
"O hail, dear Mother of my Lord!
God's coming through your singing Heart,
My Babe is leaping, like a hart."

The Inn door closed, there is no place,
Just lowly ones and beasts have space.
"All glory to our Infant King!"
The angels and the shepherds sing.

He walks among His own while here,
To find true open hearts that care.

He opens closed doors with His Grace,
To bring His Light to our dark place!

Upon a cross He does depart,
A sword pierced open His great Heart.
From stone-sealed tomb, to Life, He Rose,
To open wide the doors sin closed

"The doors! The doors!"[10] We hear them say,
The deacons in their fine array,
"Let us close them, lest the Spirit's Fire
Consumes the people and the choir."

Enclosed, now safe, in Bread and Wine,
His Fiery Presence, so Divine,
Into our open hearts He comes,
He is 'open door' for everyone.

What do the 'doors' of flesh conceal?
What does the human heart reveal?
This Flesh and Heart He's made His own.
His Presence in our lives is known.

What lies behind closed doors, we see,
In every land, on every street?
Hearts full of flaming love or hate.
Lives full of pain or joy so great.

"No more barred doors!" Lift the cry.
"The King of Glory's coming nigh!"
Now, open all your closed hearts wide.wHis Presence is
our Paradise!
"Here I am! I stand at the door and knock."
Rev. 3:20

---

[10] *Chant from St. John Chrysostom Liturgy.*

"Do not be afraid, Mary, for you have found favor with God.
Behold, you will conceive in your womb and bear a son,
and you will name him Jesus.
Mary said to the angel, "How will this be, since I am a virgin?"
The angel answered, "The Holy Spirit will come upon you,
and the power of the Most High will overshadow you.
Therefore, the child to be born will be holy,
and he will be called the Son of God.
And behold, your cousin Elizabeth in her old age
has also conceived a son,
and she who was called barren is now in her sixth month,
for nothing will be impossible for God."
Then Mary said, "Behold, I am the servant of the Lord.
Let it be done to me according to your word."
Luke 1:30-31, 34-38

ANNUNCIATION

MARY!
Child of Abraham,
Daughter of Israel,
House of David,
Lover of Yahweh.
Beloved of the Father.

Gabriel's coming
Now announcing:
"You are the honor,
You are the glory of your people,
Holy Virgin Mary." [11]

---

[11] *Dies, Lucien. Come Lord Jesus,* Song: " You Are the Honor." Chicago: World
Library Publications, *1981.*

You, are "full of grace!"[12]
Quickened by the Spirit,
Pregnant with God,
Weighted with the Word,
Bearer of the Promise.

Beautiful longing,
Loving waiting,
Humble openness,
Listening presence,
Gentle surrender!
FIAT! [13]

---

[12] Luke *1:28,* paraphrased.

[13] Latin for "let it be done."

ALL SHALL BE WELL

In His Gospel,
Matthew names
Your family tree.[14]
The branches of
Abraham and Moses,
Ruth and David,
Joseph and Mary.
Show grace and beauty,
But the branches weak
With treachery and sin,
Far outnumber them.

You, the Divine Son,
Came from a messiness,
Not unlike our own.
That helps,
When we find
In our own life,
And of those we love,
Frailty, pain and even sin.
Your sainted Juliana heard You say,
"All shall be well, and
All shall be well, and
All manner of things shall be well."[15]
If we only allow our branches,
To be grafted onto You,
Savior of our Family Tree.

---

[14] *Matthew 1.*

[15] Norwich, Juliana. *Revelations of Divine Love.* Chapter 27. Image. New York. 1977.

"When Elizabeth heard Mary's greeting,
the baby leaped in her womb.
Then Elizabeth was filled with the Holy Spirit,
and she exclaimed with a loud cry,
'Blessed are you among women,
and blessed is the fruit of your womb.
And why am I so greatly favored that the mother
of my Lord should visit me?
For behold, the moment that the sound of your greeting
reached my ears,
the child in my womb leaped for joy.
And blessed is she who believed that what the Lord
has said to her will be fulfilled.'"
Luke 1:41-45

THEOTOKOS

Theotokos, [16]
God Bearer!
Life quickens within,
Listen and feel,
The Word,
Gently and lovingly awaken, [17]
Sense the quiet power,
Of His movements
And exclaim!
Bring forth,
The Word
In loving presence,
To make Life
Leap for joy,
In another.

---

[16] Greek for God Bearer, title given to Mary the Mother of Jesus at the Council of Ephesus, in 431 AD, which confirmed the belief that Jesus is True God and True Man against the heresy of Nestorius.

[17] From poem by St. John of the Cross. "Living Flame of Love," see Appendix C.

EVICT ME

"He must increase, but I must decrease." [18]

You leapt,
In His Presence, John,
And your heart knew,
That there was room
For only One.
The task of moving out,
So, He could move in,
had begun.

"He must increase, but I must decrease."

You discovered the secret, Mary,
At the angel's word
You surrendered,
Taken over by the Spirit,
The Word grew in your womb,
The flesh He bore was yours,
We look at you, Mary,
And you bid us see only Him.

"He must increase, but I must decrease."

I want to surrender, Father.
Long ago, I gave up the lease on my life,
And You began moving in,
But it is so hard to let go of what is mine,
I cling to the spaces and places,
Of my small heart,

---

[18] *John 3:30.*

Though the vast palace of Yours
Awaits me.

Come, Spirit of God,
Evict me!
And You, Jesus
Increase in me, I plead.

The Father desires that His Word become Incarnate in you.
By the power of His Spirit may you be able to say,
"...it is no longer I who live, but it is Christ who lives in me."
Gal. 2:20

WITH GOD

God is growing big in me,
Like a woman in her ninth month,
This condition determines,
What I can and cannot do.

I am 'with God.'[19]
I cannot help,
But be aware of Him,
As I go about my daily life.

He is with me,
As I talk to my sister on the phone,
Visit a homebound parishioner,
Pack lunches for the homeless,
Write a letter to a friend,
Embrace my husband in love.

In quiet moments,
I wrap myself round,
This Hidden Presence,
Drawn, by the compelling Life,
Within me.

God is growing big in me.

---

[19] Paraphrasing a beautiful expression that was once part of our culture when referring to a pregnant woman: "She is with child."

"But we hold this treasure in earthen vessels,
that the surpassing power may be of God and not from us."
2 Cor. 4:7

HIS TIME

I wait gently,
His time to come in me,
Light growing steadily,
In my darkness,
My heart womb
Full of Being,
My whole self,
Throbbing with a Life,
So much a part of me,
But not my own,
A Life that needs so much,
My own to grow.

In pain,
My heart labors,
Christ to bear,
In giving,
My life yields to death,
And death to Life,
And when at last,
My heart womb
Is quickened by Another,
And my darkness,
Has fled before the
Dawn of Day,
His time will come in me,
Gently,
Christ will be born again.

"If you want, the Virgin will come walking down the road
pregnant with the Holy and say,
'I need shelter for the night.
Please take me inside your heart, my time is so close.'"[20]

LIVE OUT

The Father's Word
Pierced through our darkness,
He came as a child,
In the stillness of night.

He seeks now again,
To walk here among us.
Into our lives,
He sends fullness of Light.

Your life is gifted,
For His own purpose.
Welcome His Spirit,
Live out His Presence!

---

[20] From poem by St. John of the Cross, "Advent Poem," see Appendix *C*.

"He came to his own, but his own did not accept him."
John 1:11

THE INN

Amid the empty laughter
Of holiday raucous,
A knock upon the door.

"Go away!
Don't disturb our celebration!
We're all filled up.
(With food and drink and greedy gifts)!"

At His coming,
Will He find you,
Too full,
To welcome Him?

CHOOSE LIFE

Little One, Peaceful One,
Gentle healing from above,
Poor ones see, rejoice, and know,
That You are here, because of Love.

Mighty ones, proud-heart ones,
Resent Your gentle Presence here,
They cannot bear the weight of Love,
Your healing touch is what they fear.

"We must worship!" "We must kill!"
Two ways the world responded then,
God's Power in Your weakness seen,
Reveals the heart in each of them.

"We must change." "We must deny."
No indifference, to the sight
Of Your humble Presence here,
Come to us, this Silent Night.

THREE WISHES

I wish you Joseph,
Loving strong one,
God's protection,
Listening silence
Hearing Spirit speak,
In painful openness.

I wish you Mary,
Loving waiting one,
Cup overflowing,
God spilling out,
From Spirit-filled
Virgin emptiness.

I wish you Jesus,
Loving poor one,
Hope Incarnate,
God going forth,
From Godhead's glory,
To live our weakness.

"Because the crowd had heard that he had performed this sign,
they went out to meet him.
So, the Pharisees said to one another,
'As you see, we are getting nowhere.
The entire world has gone after him.'"
John 12:18-19

WELCOME JESUS

You visited our life, Jesus.
Poor hosts that we are,
We gave You a 'living space'
No better than our own.

You shared our bread and wine,
and weakness,
You knew our struggle,
To find a bit of light and warmth
Amidst the darkness and cold,
Of these human accommodations.

Yet the poor place of
Your 'human being'
Was filled with glory and Love.
The warmth of Your Presence
Drew others near,
And Your life-space became,
The gathering place,
For those seeking someplace
To call home.

You visited our life, Jesus,
And changed the 'living room' of all.
Becoming Yourself
The Home,
The Host,
The Welcome.

BAPTISM

He was, oh, so beautiful!
In His passing by,
A wave of tenderness
Washed over me,
And I knew joy!
I saw Him, and yet,
I saw Him not,
For He was a clear vessel,
Hollowed out and empty –
No, not empty, filled,
With a Life,
That was greater than
That fragile human form
Could contain.

He was cup running over,
Bubbling fountain spilling
Into a thirsty world,
Refreshing
Our parched spirits,
Restoring hearts
Grown dry and hard,
And His words were like
A mountain stream,

"Come to Me, I will refresh you,
I will give you living waters,
That you will never thirst again,
For I have come
That you may have Life,
And have it to the full." [21]

"'Come and see a man who told me everything I have ever done.
Could this be the Christ?'
And so, they departed from the town and
made their way to see him."
John 4:29-30

---

[21] *John 3:10-14, John 10:10, Matthew 11:28.*

HIS HEART SPEAKS

It burns in me like Fire,
This knowledge of My Father,
This awareness of His Love!
My heart and mind are so full,
With whom
Can I share this blazing?

My Abba?
Yes, Joseph knew,
As we sat together in the evening
Studying the Torah,
Chanting His Psalms,
Knowing the Divine Presence,
As we prayed together at night.

My Ema? [22]
What joy!
Just to walk with her
In the cool of the morning,
In the silence of the hills,
Praising the Holy One,
Sharing His Love.
She knew the secrets of My Heart.

How I miss them,
And my home,
In Nazareth!
But I must walk these hills,
And shepherd My people
In their poverty and pain.

---

[22] Aramaic for mama or mother.

How My Heart longs to share the joy
Of My Father's Love with them.
But their hearts and minds
Can only take a little at a time.
So, like My Father
Feeds the birds of the air,
With crumbs
Of His tremendous Love.
I feed them,
With stories,
That is all their hearts can stand,
For now.

But what do I do
With the Fire?
Even my disciples are not ready.
Except for one,
John.
Not that I love him more.
But my Father
Has readied his heart and mind,
So that I am not alone
In this knowing.
He can read
The secrets of My Heart.
He burns with them,
And with him
I can share the Fire!

John 14: 8-10: "Philip said to him, 'Lord, show us the Father,
it will be enough for us.' Jesus answered, 'Have I been with
you all this time, Philip, and you still do not know me?
Whoever has seen me has seen the Father. How can you say,
'Show us the Father'? Do you not believe that
I am in the Father and the Father is in me? The words
that I speak to you I do not speak on my own.
The Father who dwells in me is doing his works.'"

OUR FATHER'S LOVE

I love you,
Like a Voice in the heart,
Promising Abraham
My love forever.
Like a Voice in a dream,
Telling Joseph
He will save My people.
Like a Voice in a Burning Bush
Saying,
"I have heard the cry of My People."
Like a Voice in a cloud
Proclaiming,
"I will be your God and you will be My People."
Like the Voice of My Prophets,
Foretelling a Messiah,
A Savior.

Like the Voice of an Angel
Announcing to Mary,
"You will conceive, bear a Son,
And name Him Jesus...
He will save His people from their sins."
Like a Voice in the wilderness,
Crying out,

"Prepare the Way" for My Son.
Like a Baby in Bethlehem,
My Son,
Who came to share
Your life and your death.

Like a wild Shepherd seeking,
The one lost sheep,
Leaving the ninety-nine.
Like an anxious woman
Searching,
High and low,
For a lost coin.
Like a loving Father
Waiting and waiting,
For His lost son's return.
Like a Samaritan
Binding the wounds,
Of an injured enemy.

Like a Friend eating,
With tax collectors and sinners.
Like a Healer who preaches,
And heals and loves to the end.
Like a Master washing
The feet of His disciples.
Like a Lover giving Himself,
To be consumed, in the Bread
And Wine of Eucharist.
Like a Savior, My Beloved Son,
Opening His arms wide,
And dying on the Cross for you.

My Son told you,
"Whoever has seen Me
Has seen the Father."[23]
This is how I, Your Father,
Loves you.
Can you hear
My Voice in your heart?
"I am your loving Father."

"My Beloved Father, Thy will be done on earth as it is in Heaven. Be Thou my Father. Be always my Eternal Father. Do not leave my soul. Do not abandon me. Do not leave me out of your sight, my Father, for I am your child, whom you have created to please You, to adore You, to honor You, living my days as You have given me the freedom to live them."[23]

---

[23] "The Fiat of the Eternal Father," a morning prayer from the writings of a mystic.

"Do you not have a saying, 'Four months more, and then comes the harvest'?
I tell you, open your eyes and look at the fields;
already they are white for the harvest."
John 4:35

SPOKEN FORTH

Seed-word seeking soul-ground,
Pulsing with promised power,
Two-edged sword, seed,

```
    r              up,
    o              g
    o              n
    t              i
    i              s
    n              i
    g              r
  down            and
```

Breaking through the selfish soil,
So long impacted in my heart.
Let my Lazarus-like being,
Hear the Word:
"Come forth!"
"Unbind!"
"Go free!" [24]

---

[24] *John 11*:43-44 paraphrased.

"The kingdom of heaven may be compared
to a man who sowed good seed in his field.
While everyone was asleep, his enemy came,
sowed weeds among the wheat, and then went away.
When the wheat sprouted and ripened,
the weeds also appeared.
Let them both grow together until the harvest. ...
At harvest time, I will tell the reapers,
'Collect the weeds first and tie them in bundles to be burned.
Then gather the wheat into my barn.'"
Matthew 13:24-26,30

HEART HARVEST

Harvest my heart, Lord!
Weed wild seed sown,
Seed wheat now grown,
Deep down within me.

Sever me now, Lord!
From earthbound rooting,
And tangled up growing,
With Your Hand sort me.

Gather me now, Lord!
My errant heart leanings,
Human love seeking,
With Your Look chasten.

Winnow me now, Lord!
Life chaff for burning,
Love seed for sowing,
Heart field now empty.

Fill me up, Holy!
Seed Word full growing,
Spirit Flame glowing
Father Love showing.

"Amen, amen, I say to you, unless a grain of wheat
falls into the earth and dies, it remains just a grain of wheat.
However, if it dies, it bears much fruit."
John 12:24

ONE GRAIN

Sacred Wheat Seed,
Beloved Son sown,
In Mary ground, grown.
Crowds taste and see,
And long for more.
One grain alone
Cannot provide,
You must be sown.

Husk stripped away.
Nail furrow, dug deep,
In pain covered ground,
Blood-watered seed,
Is buried now.
We've tearfully sown,
Sacred Wheat Seed,
One of our own.

Sacred Wheat Seed,
Beloved Son sown,
In our ground, grown.
Death has released,
Life power within.
In Your Rising,
Seed of Abundant Life,
In us is sown.

SEVEN SACRED WORDS [25]

"Let your attitude be identical to that of Christ Jesus.
Though he was in the form of God,
he did not regard equality with God
as something to be grasped. Rather, he emptied himself,
taking the form of a slave, being born in human likeness.
Being found in appearance as a man, he humbled himself,
and became obedient to death, even death on a cross.
Because of this, God greatly exalted him and
bestowed on him the name
that is above all other names, so that at the name of Jesus
every knee should bend of those in heaven and on earth
and under the earth,
and every tongue should proclaim to the
glory of God the Father:
Jesus Christ is Lord."
Philippians 2:5-11

---

[25] *Based on Luke 23:34, Luke 23:43, John 19:26-27, Mt. 27:46, Mark 15:34,*
John 19:28, John 19:30, Luke 23:46.

Father Forgive Them

Hear Me, Father, please forgive them,
They know not what they do.
Lost, alone, without a shepherd,
They wandered far from You.
Caught in a dark anxiety,
They heard a stranger's voice.
Crippled by their gnawing fear,
They made an awful choice.
"It's better now" the High-Priest said,
"That this One dies upon the Cross,
Lest the nation and the people,
Be now, forever lost."
I am their Shepherd and their Lord,
My love has paid the cost.
I will draw them to my wounded Heart,
I will rescue all the lost.

This Day

His heart was open to My grace,
Despite the pain upon his face.
When Gestas cursed and taunted Me,
He spoke up and defended Me.

"We suffer justly for our sins,
This Holy Man is innocent!
Jesus, my Lord, remember me,
When in Your Kingdom, You are free."

Look at Me, Dismas, my dear friend,
To you I say, Amen! Amen!
This day, I promise you will be,
This day, in paradise with Me.

Behold

I look with tender, grieving love,
On You, my dearest Mother,
Behold, Your loving, dying Son,
To You, I give another.
Take him now, into Your Heart.
Dear John, behold your Mother!
In pain, in love and one in Heart,
You will make your home together,
You will find Me close beside you there,
For I will leave you never.
Into this Home, your Heart in Mine,
Bring all the world together.

My God! My God!

My God! My God! I cry to Thee,
Why have You now abandoned Me?
Deep darkness hides Your light from Me.
Your loving Face I cannot see.
In anguish, I behold their sins,
Their pain and violence deep within,
The suffering child, the tortured man,
The woman's pain – My enemy's hand.
He pierced My Mother's Heart in grief,
And from Her pain there is no relief.
My God! My God! I cry to Thee.
I know!
You will not abandon them or Me!

I Thirst

I thirst, but not for water,
Or the blood of the vine.
I thirst, and for this thirst,
I give my life, Divine,

I give My Life to quench the thirst,
That tortures humankind,
And now I thirst, that only you,
Give Me your life for Mine.

It Is Finished

My blood is falling to the ground,
My agony's unending,
The sky is darkening all around,
The very earth is splitting.
I hear the muted sobs of grief,
My heart breaks for My Mother.
The pain – excruciating, deep,
O, where are You, My Father?
Great terror seeps into My Soul,
My Body trembles, shudders!
Where are those who followed Me,
Who shared My Love, My Supper?
I die alone upon this Cross,
But all I've done, won't come to naught!
One Faithful One, She gave Me birth!
My death has wedded Heaven and earth –
It is finished!

Into Your Hands!

Into Your loving Hands I fall,
I yield, My Soul, My Life, My all.
You are My God, My Father true,
You walked with Me My whole life through.
I trusted and You did not fail,
Even in death, You love Me still!
The darkness grows and fills My Soul,
The pain of flesh now takes its toll.
The web of death falls over Me,
I hear all anguished cries to Thee,
My Heart is filled with dreadful fear,
Receive My Spirit, Father dear.

Pieta in St. Bernard Church, Mt. Lebanon, PA

HOLY SATURDAY

Saturday — the day between,
The nothing day — the no thing day,
No trials or scourging, no crying out or dying,
To even talk about it seems useless,
Because that was yesterday,
And today is just today, taking us to tomorrow.

Saturday — the day between,
The nothing day — the no thing day,
No alleluias or Eucharist, no stone rolled back or rising to glory,
Even the heart refrains from thinking it,
because that is tomorrow,
And today is just today, taking us to tomorrow.

Waiting day — in which all waitings,
Are rolled up into one intense moment,

The music is about to begin,
The curtain is about to rise,
The door is about to be opened,
The plane is ready for take-off,
The phone is going to ring,
The buds are about to blossom,
The rose is almost opened,
The birds are about to return,
The butterfly is struggling out of its cocoon,
The chick is pecking at the eggshell,
The baby is about to be born,
The words are going to be said,
The wound is almost healed,
The sun is coming up,
The dawn is finally here!
The *stone* is going to be rolled away!

The moment of expectation,
That intense moment of life
Filled with the unspeakable joy,
Of knowing what will surely be,
That moment when one's whole being,
Is poised in complete openness,
An openness into which God can come!

By Your dying, Lord Jesus,
You have taken us into the
Hollowed places of Your Wounds.
You have hidden us there today,
And we wait in the peaceful darkness,
For growth and healing to come.
Nourished by Your Holy Body and Blood,
As a child is nourished in its mother's womb,
We wait to be born tomorrow!

"Now Thomas, called the Twin, who was one of the Twelve,
was not with the rest when Jesus came.
When the other disciples told him,
'We have seen the Lord,' he replied,
'Unless I see the mark of the nails on his hands
and put my finger
into the place where the nails pierced
and insert my hand into his side,
I will not believe.'"
John 20:24-25

THOMAS-LIKE

"Risen?"
"With us?"
My pain walls seeing.
Tending wounds of my own making,
And of others.
My heart struggles.

Dare I believe?
When all of me cries out,
To touch the wounding of Your Flesh.
Then my mind will stop the probing
Of the one now speaking hope.

"Look" You said,
"At him who is speaking,
Of a wounding and a healing.
Here, in him, I stand before you.
See the Glory of My Wounds now.
See and touch, in him, My Flesh now.
In his presence, I am with you.
In his weakness, I am Risen.
See in him My promise given,
All your sins have been forgiven.
Rise in Me to new Life's Glory,
In your weakness find My Story."

"And he said to them,
'Thus, it is written that the Christ would suffer and
on the third day rise from the dead,
and that in his name repentance and forgiveness of sins
are to be proclaimed to all nations,
beginning from Jerusalem.
You are witnesses to all these things.
And behold, I am sending upon you
the Gift promised by my Father.
Therefore, stay here in the city until
you have been clothed with power from on high.'"
Luke 24:46-49

PENTECOST

Their eyes opened to new vision,
Now transformed, they face the world,
He had given them a mission,
With the Power to endure.
All they were, is now held captive,
In a Strength that sets them free,
Having but one Word to give now,
They go forth to plant the Seed.
As they walk, they see the growth,
Of His Spirit in their lives,
There is an echo in their hearts,
Of a Voice with power and might.

"I the Vine and you, the branches,
Growing, in my Father's world.
Keep my Words, give all the chance,
To know the love, I have for them.
Live on in Me, as I in you,
Without My Strength you will never be,
My Body is your daily food,
As daily, too, you die for Me.
My Father's Will is now your life,
Lived out in love, as Mine has been.
My Name is yours, you have the right,
Ask all, and all, is yours in Me." [26]

And now, my heart, has heard the Voice,
Transforming life and love in me.
Daily walking with the Spirit,
I go forth to plant the Seed.

---

[26] *John 15-16.*

CHAPTER THREE

Creation Speaks

*"Ever since the creation of the world
the invisible attributes God's eternal power and divine nature
have been clearly understood and perceived
through the things he has made."
Romans 1:20*

The Milky Way

"The heavens proclaim the glory of God;
the firmament shows forth the work of his hands.
One day imparts that message to the next,
and night conveys that knowledge to night.
All this occurs without speech or utterance;
no voice can be heard.
Yet their message goes forth throughout the earth,
and their words to the ends of the world."
Psalm 19:2-4

UNION

I look at the night,
Darkness seeps down
And envelops my soul,
In profound stillness.
Out of that darkness,
Millions of stars,
With magnetic force,
Draw my soul upward,
In the vast heavens,
My spirit experiences.
Eternity,
I gaze at the night,
And find,
Union with God.

"The moon is a well-known and ancient symbol of Mary,
the Mother of God.
Just as the moon reflects the light of the sun,
so, the splendor of the Immaculate Virgin Mary
reflects the light of the true Sun, God himself.
And because Mary brought this light,
Jesus Christ, who is God, to us,
she can help us in developing a relationship with God."[27]

VIGIL

In the star-studded night sky,
The full moon now gently shines,
Mary's maternal vigil,
Over Her weary children in time.

She will keep Her loving vigil,
Until all earth's darkness gives way,
To Her Risen Savior Son,
Leading us to Eternal Day!

---

[27] Burke, Roderic "Mary to the Moon," *Missio Immaculatae.* May/June 2023, Vol. 19.

THE WOMAN

Morning comes in softly,
Quietly stepping through the mist,
Her garments rustling gently,
From the breeze that never rests.

From her golden head there falls
Strands of sunlight on the earth,
Piercing life's darkest halls,
Taking sadness leaving mirth.

From her lips moist with dew
Comes a song of various trills,
Awakens in the soul anew,
A prayer, a prayer at will.

O come, come thou Woman of morn,
To the tempest of life's test,
Soothe this soul of sorrow born,
With thy sweet tender caress.

MY BLUE HEAVEN

Mary covers this place today,
With Her blue mantle sky,
Full of billowing white clouds of grace,
A fitting setting, for Her Son's sun,
Lighting the world,
With penetrating rays
Of His Presence.

"Where can I flee from your Presence?
If I ascend to the heavens, You are there...*"[28]*

Why would I flee
This encompassing Love,
That has carried me my whole life,
Like a mother
Carrying her child?

I nestle close, O God,
To Your Heart,
So, like the Heart of Your Mother,
Nothing can touch me here,
Though storms rage around
And within me,
"All is Grace."[29]

I need not be concerned,
If my weakness shows.
An infant cares not, that it is helpless,
It cares only for the arms,
And the Love,
That hold it fast.

"Like a weaned child held in its mother's arms,
So is my soul within me."[30]

---

[28] *Psalm* 139:7-8, see Appendix D.

[29] Quote from Saint Therese of Lisieux, see Appendix E.

[30] *Psalm* 131:2.

TOO CLOSE

This world, O God,
Is Your Face,
And I crawl all over it,
But I cannot see You,
You are too close to me.

I walk up and down,
The wrinkles of Your cheeks,
And climb the furrows
Of Your forehead.
Your beard and hair are the forests,
Where I wander in delight.
Your whistling is heard,
In the chirping of the birds.
My heart is warmed,
As You speak to me
In the heat of the day,
And in the breeze, all around,
Your sweet breath cools me,

But I cannot see You,
You are too close to me.

As You gaze at me
Through the day,
I see my world,
And all things in it,
By the light
Streaming from Your Eyes.
The closing of Your eyelids
Brings on the night,
And Your Arms of Love
Enfold me in darkness.

I fall asleep,
On the softness of Your cheek,
Finding peace in Your Presence.

This world, O God, is Your Face,
But I cannot see You,
You are too close to me.

WATERFALLS

The Creative Love of God
Fills our world.
It cascades grace,
Over my willing heart,
Stripping and shaping
A masterpiece,
A heaven for Himself.
He tumbles into
This resting place often,
As He makes His rounds,
Searching and calling
From the torrents to His children.

"I love you!
I say it
With every drop
Of these flowing waters.
I want to fill you
With My Life
And My Joy
Without bounds!
Come Home to My Love!"

Ithaca Falls, Ithaca, NY

OUR SEA GOD

Wear me down, Lord,
By the relentless waves of Your Love.
Crashing upon my stony heart.
Smooth out the resistance,
Leaving nothing to impede
Your inflowing Presence.
Hollow out a space,
Into which,
You can freely come and go.
And when, I am made,
Quite smooth and small
And hollow,
Carry me away with You,
Claim me as Your own,
As the sea does the land,
And hold me in the depths.
Of Your Heart.

SOUL-TIDE

Soul-sea, shaped
By that in which it rests,
Depths of being, stilled,
In the seabed,
Of Divinity.

Soul-tide, drawn within,
By the Father's Hand,
Away from time's shore,
Into eternity,
To be filled with Love.

The living Spirit of God,
Makes my love's rest active,
As Christ,
The Incarnate One,
Walks the sea of me.

My soul-wave, drawn by Love,
Back upon the shore of life,
Brings Living Water
And His Love,
To all that be.

GOD ALONE

The depths and breadth of the ocean,
Can never fill the space,
Within my heart.
Its waves crash upon my shore,
Cutting ever deeper into my core,
Carving out a deep abyss.
Flowing in and out.

The waters satisfy my daily thirst,
But leave me longing for more.
God alone,
Can satisfy the longings of my heart.
"As a deer longs for running streams,
so my soul longs for you, O God.
My soul thirsts for God, the living God.
When shall I come to behold the face of God?" [31]

---

[31] *Psalm 42:2-3.*

"But ask the animals, and they will teach you;
ask the birds of the air, and they will inform you.
Ask the reptiles on earth, and they will instruct you,
or let the fish of the sea enlighten you.
Which of all these is unaware
that the hand of God has done this?
'In God's hand is the soul of every living thing
and the breath of all mankind.'"
Job 12:7-10

THE DEER

The deer stepped cautiously,
Into the clearing,
Leaving the sheltered coolness
Of the trees.
To feel the sun
Full upon her back.

A twig snaps,
Her heart skips a beat.
She knows,
She has been seen.
Vulnerable,
She holds herself tense,
Heart beating wildly in her fright,
Eyes staring into the eyes of the seer,
"Are you friend or foe?" She asks,
Her whole being held,
In a balance of trust.

Then in a flash
And a bounding leap
She is gone,
So, like a soul's shyness,
New, to God's Presence.

"This is the generation of those who seek him,
who seek the face of the God of Jacob."
Psalm 24:6

HIDDEN THERE

Walking in the woods
I seek a glimpse,
Of the deer living there.
They are so much like
My elusive God.
I know He is near,
I sense Him watching,
From the thicket of my life,
But my eyes fail to see Him,
Hidden there.

Only when I patiently
Wait and watch,
With the eyes of my heart
Seeking,
My anxiety silenced,
Do I catch a fleeting Image.
For a moment, His eyes meet mine,
And I know,
I have been caught by Him,
Hidden there.
"Truly you are a God who is hidden,
O God of Israel, the Savior." [32]

---

[32] *Isaiah 45:15*

RUNNING FREE

Lassie leaps for joy,
As we head out the door,
To walk and run is her delight.
I feel guilty as I rein her in,
But she forgives me the leash,
And enjoys what she can.

How, unlike God I am,
He lets me run free, He trusts me,
Though He knows I will stray,
Wander far, and forget, for a while,
Where my home is.
He patiently waits,
As I chase after
Fleeting joys and empty pleasures.

From time to time,
He calls my name,
And looks down the road,
To see if I am coming home.
When He suspects that I am lost,
And longing for Him,
He sends His wild Spirit after me.
She tethers me with Love,
And leads me home,
To leap joyfully,
Into His waiting arms.

IF I LET HER

In the morning,
If I let Her,
God,
Leaps into my arms,
And licks my nose.

SERPENT

Serpent, earth's creature,
Your sister am I,
Welcome!

Much maligned are you,
"It's evil!" they cry,
Fearing.

Yet, humbly you live,
Hugging the earth's floor,
Reverence.

Bearing your nature,
Praising Creator,
Freely.

Genesis' story
Marked you as tempter,
Punished.[33]

Exodus' telling,
Proclaimed you as healer,
Raised up.[34]

Type of the Savior,
All shame transformed now,
Through Him.

Serpent, earth's creature,
Your sister am I!

---

[33] *Genesis 3:14.*

[34] *Numbers 21:8-9.*

"However, the Advocate, the Holy Spirit,
whom the Father will send in my name,
will teach you everything
and remind you of all that I have said to you."
John 14:26

HOW DO I KNOW YOU?

Overshadowing Presence,
Voice of the Prophets,
Consuming Fire,
Whispering Sound,
Eagle carrying Its young aloft.

Gentle Dove,
Spouse of the Virgin,
Giver of Life,
Father's Anointing,
Brooding Hen gathering Its chicks.

Almighty Power,
Whirling Wind,
First Gift of the Father,
Holy Wisdom kindling hearts,
Tongues of Fire alighting our minds,

Teacher of Truth,
Treasury of blessings,
Granter of forgiveness,
Comforter given as Paraclete,
Advocate for my defense.

Sea of my being,
Voice in my heart crying "Abba."
Strength and joy of my spirit,
Grace in my soul remembering,
The all-encompassing Love of my God.

Creator renewing all
With Eternal Divine Love,
The Breathing of God,
Present everywhere,
Filling all things with Holiness,
Holy Spirit of God.

DESIRE

Winter trees,
Naked,
In your desire for Spring,
Your stark beauty
Speaks remembrance,
Of a former longed-for glory.
Unashamedly,
You raise your arms,
In supplication,
To our Creator,
Longing for the sun's
Penetrating rays,
To awaken you.
Knowing your barrenness,
Is rooted,
In the earth's
Deep source of life,
You wait in hope,
For the stirring
Of His Life,
Deep within.

*"Blessed are those who trust in the LORD and whose
hope is the LORD.
They will be like a tree planted by the water
that spreads out its roots to the stream.
When the heat comes, it does not fear; its leaves stay green.
It is not concerned in a year of drought,
and it never fails to bear fruit."
Jeremiah 17:7-8*

Sunrise at Gethsemani Abbey, KY

TREES OF GOD

"Little Flowers of God."
Thus, St. Thérèse of Lisieux,
Would describe young lives,
Given over to God,
Like Tarcisius, Goretti and Acutis.[35]
Their souls bloomed early,
For a brief time,
Gave off a fragrance,
Then yielded,
To the Son's compelling Presence,
And died.

But what of us seasoned souls?
Harkening to His call, some early, some late,
But faithfully following day in and day out,
Bearing the heat, the storms, the drought,
The ebb and flow of Presence and absence.
"Lord, have mercy on me, a sinner."
"Let me never be lukewarm." [36]
I cry,
As I reach into a silent sky.

With branches sometimes bare, sometimes full,
We age seventy, eighty, even ninety years,
Waiting, hoping, suffering, not knowing,
"Do I please Him?
Have I done His Will?
What do all these years mean to Him?"

---

[35] Young Saints, see Appendix E.

[36] Jesus Prayer of Eastern Spirituality (see Appendix F) and reference to
Revelation 3:16:"As it is, since you are lukewarm, neither cold nor hot, I
will spit you out of my mouth."

I name us,
"Trees of God."
Unlike flowers,
We are rooted deep,
In earth's joys and pains
And responsibilities to keep,
But always reaching heavenward,
Longing for the day,
When harvested by the Lord,
Our rings will tell the story,
Of long lives led in His Presence,
Alive through Grace,
Like John, Drexel, and Sheen, [37]
But scarred by this world's darkness,
As Jesus was scarred,
On a Tree,
On Calvary.

---

[37] Older Saints, see Appendix E.

*"Absorb my heart, Lord, from all things under heaven,
by the power of Your Love."*[38]

GENTLE LOVER

You are a gentle Lover, O God!
Your shy Presence,
Fills my days and my nights,
Your tenderness holds me fast.

When I suddenly glimpse You,
Amid a busy day,
My heart leaps with desire,
To see the wondrous Beauty of Your Face.

When I feel Your Love wash over me,
In the coolness of a soft rain,
My dry spirit thirsts,
To drink the fullness of Your Grace.

When I hear Your Words whisper,
In a gentle breeze across my face,
I long to hear,
The full power of Your Voice.

As I sit down for prayer,
You turn me towards You,
With a delicate touch of Your Spirit,
And I burn for Your embrace.

When Your Image flits across my mind,
As I drift off to sleep,
I search in the night,

---

[38] From "Absorbeat Prayer" by St. Francis Assisi, see Appendix G.

To meet You face to face,
Walking in my dreams.

You make no demands,
Yet, You claim
My heart,
My soul,
My mind.

You are a gentle Lover, O God,
Your shy Presence,
Fills my days and my nights,
And Your tenderness holds me fast.

MY HEART BEHOLDS

A myriad of cares
Draw me from Your Presence.
Yet in faith I find You
In a hundred places,
a thousand faces:

Faithful love,
Nature's beauty,
Unwanted pain,
Gentle friendship,
Enduring strength,
Human weakness,
Searching hope,
Struggling faith,
Daily joys,
Days of darkness,
In life, in death,
In the deep-down core,
Of everything that is,
Somehow,
You are there.

Though my mind does not attend You,
My heart beholds You,
Divine Presence.

"Surely it is a wonderful grace to receive the Sacraments.
When God does not permit it, it is good too!
Everything is grace!"[39]

HOLY EARTH

Holy Earth,
Our Creator fashioned you,
With great Love,
To be our home.
His command
Filled you with power,
To bring forth life in abundance,
The beauty of your flowers,
And food to nourish
All His creatures.
He hid treasures within you,
For our discovery.
He fashioned us,
From the very minerals
Of which you are formed.

You felt the press
Of our Savior's feet upon you,
As He walked your roads,
A Man on a mission.
We call His country
The Holy Land.
You cradled Him,
In sleep on His journeys,
And as He fell,
On the way to His death.

---

[39] St, Therese of Lisieux. See Appendix E.

You became the Chalice,
To receive His Blood,
That Good Friday,
You are the 'Holy Grail,'
We need seek no further.
"Remember that you are 'earth' [40]
And to the 'earth' you shall return."
As I walk upon you,
I find Communion,
Holy Earth.

\

---

[40] Paraphrase of Ash Wednesday Liturgy antiphon "Remember that you are dust and unto dust you shall return" Roman Missal.

HOLY WIND

Holy Wind,
Breathed into Adam
With great Love,
By our Creator,
You became air and wind,
To fill my world.
Birds are held aloft by you,
As they sing to their Creator.
You gently caress me,
On a warm summer day,
Or proclaim His formidable power,
In a stormy sea at night.
Thunder roars through you,
As lightning bolts crash to earth,
And you lift trees and homes like toys
In your powerful grasp.

On the night of Christ's birth,
The Angels filled you,
With heavenly music.
You were made holy,
As you filled our Savior's lungs,
The Breath of God!
You carried His Words, His Prayers,
His Sobs and His Song.
Your storm did His bidding,
When He commanded calm.
He breathed you into His priests,
As Holy Power to forgive,
And returned you, His Breath,
As a Gift to the Father.
You are a sign of the Holy Spirit.
Every breath I take,
Becomes Communion,
Holy Wind.

HOLY FIRE

Holy Fire,
With great Love,
Our Creator harnessed you
In our sun.
You give warmth and light,
To my earthly home.
Making possible
Life upon this earth,
For all its inhabitants.
You silently burn
At its core,
And erupt violently,
In our volcanoes.
You are God's Power
That serves, purifies.
Or destroys,
The inner energy
Of every living being.

You warmed Jesus on cold nights,
During His life in our world,
And cooked the food that nourished Him.
You are the outward sign,
Of God's Love flaming forth,
From His Sacred Heart,
As He walked among His people.
He came to enkindle our hearts,
By His Presence,
And named us all,
'Light for the world.'
He set aflame with His Word,
The hearts of the disciples of Emmaus,
Then sent His fiery Spirit

Upon His people,
To make everyone
Burn with His Love.
Every moment in Light,
And in Love,
I find Communion,
Holy Fire.

"You sailed the sea. I was in the sea, but you did not see Me.
I was in the earth, and you walked the earth
but did not know Me.
You sinned. And all the while I was sustaining and loving you."[41]

HOLY WATER

Holy Water,
Made fruitful,
By the Spirit's hovering,
In Genesis,
You gave birth,
To a world of creatures,
From sea monsters to tiny crawfish.
You cradle the land with oceans.
You drench me in His Love
As you fall from the sky.
You are the Creator's sweet Life,
Sustenance and refreshment,
As you run through our lives,
In rivers, streams, waterfalls, and brooks.
The sea that flows through my veins
Is Living Water.

You quenched Christ's thirst,
As He lived in Galilee and Judea.
The Savior's Body sanctified you,
When you were Baptism for Him,
In the Jordan.
He sailed upon you,
On the Lake of Gennesaret.
He asked for you as gift,
From a woman in Samaria,

---

[41] Piccarreta, Louisa, Servant of God. Book of Heaven, Vol. 1 paraphrased.

And from His enemies,
As He hung dying on the cross.
You are a Holy Gift,
When I give you in His Name.
The fountain that flowed,
From His pierced Heart,
Cleanses my soul.
He promised streams of living water,
Would well up from within us.
Every sip I take,
Becomes Communion,
Holy Water.

HOLY BODY

Holy Body,
Fashioned by God
With great Love,
To house His Breath, His Life.
I was given a body,
For His purposes.
Ears to hear His Word,
Eyes to see His Beauty,
Lips to sing His Praises,
A mind to know His Truth,
Hands to work and do His Will,
A heart to experience
His Presence and His Love,
And to love Him in return,
As I show forth
That Love to all.

Mary gave a Body,
To our Savior,
A Humanity,
To clothe His Divinity.
He lived and loved,
Worked and prayed,
Suffered and died,
As I do.
Every moment and act
Of His Life and Death,
Was a Saving Act for me.
In His Resurrection
He transfigured,
His earthly Body,
And my whole life.

And having Loved me to the end
He contained His Holy Body,
In our earthly bread transformed.
He is my Holy Communion,
Holy Body.

CHAPTER FOUR

Sacramental Love

"Peace be with you," Jesus said to them again.
"As the Father has sent me, so I send you."
After saying this, he breathed on them and said,
"Receive the Holy Spirit.
If you forgive anyone's sins, they are forgiven.
If you retain anyone's sins, they are retained."
John 20:21-23

"Take and eat, this is My Body" Mt. 26:26
Father James Garvey

"A Sacrament is an outward sign, instituted by Christ
to give us Grace."[42]
Something we see, do, hear, touch, taste, receive, feel, speak.
Like water, oil, bread, wine, words, hands, heads, men, women.
Like washing, repenting, forgiving, absolving, offering,
eating, vowing, loving, ordaining, anointing.
Stuff of human life taken up by Christ,
to be Holy Signs of His ministry through His priests to our souls.
He shares His very Life with us, won for us by
His death on the Cross.

"O God, who wonderfully created the dignity of human nature
and still more wonderfully restored it,
grant, we pray, that we may share in the Divinity of Christ,
who humbled himself to share in our humanity." [43]

---

[42] Definition of Sacrament from *Baltimore Catechism*.

[43] Prayer from Christmas Mass, during the day, *Roman Missal*.

"Go, therefore, and make disciples of all nations,
baptizing them in the name of the Father and of the Son and
of the Holy Spirit."
Matthew 28:19

DIVINE ETCHINGS

I have discovered,
One of Your hobbies, God,
I keep finding Your handiwork.
You like to do etchings.

Day after day,
You bend over Your world,
Tooling away at Your Creations,
Whistling to Yourself.

You began,
When I was brought to You,
As a babe in arms,
Etching a cross on my brow,[44]
Not once, not twice,
But three times.
+++
Then You carefully marked
Each of my senses [45]
With the cross,
Consecrating my whole being
For You alone.

---

[44] Part of the ritual of a traditional Catholic Baptism when I was baptized
in 1942.

[45] *Ibid.*

Soon after, a faint outline
Of the Image of Your Son,
Appeared on my soul.
You even etched Your loving law
Deep in my being for my instruction.

Year after year You toiled away,
Deepening and refining,
With every blessing,
That faint Image,
Annihilating any other,
That might appear.
And now,
You have signed Your work,
Etching,
The Name of Jesus,
On my heart.

"Then he took bread, and after giving thanks
He broke it and gave it to them, saying,
'This is My Body, which will be given for you.
Do this in memory of Me.'
And He did the same with the cup after supper, saying,
'This cup is the new covenant in my Blood,
which will be poured out for you.'"
Luke 22:19-20

THE BODY OF CHRIST

We have in our days,
No Burning Bush,
Or Voice
Speaking from the clouds,
No lightning-written
Stone Tablets of The Law.

We have no angels telling,
Glad tidings or grim warnings,
No Voice from heaven
Naming us,
His Beloved Child.

Jesus, in His human form,
Does not announce His teachings,
From our mounts.
We see no Tongues of Fire,
No mighty winds of Spirit,
Shaking our foundations.

No —
All we have is,
Bread and Wine,

The Word,
The Priest,
And one another —
Holding in our Hearts
His last wish and command,
"Do this in remembrance of Me,"
The BODY OF CHRIST!

The Tabernacle, St. Bernard Church, Mt. Lebanon, PA

EUCHARIST FOR GOD

In the Tabernacle,
His silent Presence speaks,
Of His longing,
To be one with us.
In the dark of human elements,
He waits,
To be taken and consumed.[46]

So would my heart be Eucharist for God.

Held by faith's darkness,
In a Tabernacle of silence,
Longing,
To be one with Him,
Waiting,
To be taken and consumed.

---

[46] *The Consecrated Bread is kept in a Tabernacle, a small, usually gold-plated container on the altar in Catholic Churches. Jesus tells us in John 6:32-54 the meaning of this "Bread," His Real Presence.*

"Indeed, he was constantly with Jesus;
he bore Jesus always in his heart,
Jesus on his lips, Jesus in his ears, Jesus in his eyes,
Jesus in his hands, Jesus in every other part of his being."[47]

CONSECRATION [48]

There should not be,
Much of me
Left in this world.
For years I have come,
Open and willing,
To have the Sacred Fire
Of your Presence enter me.
Thousands of times
I have taken and eaten,
Your Sacred Body,
In Holy Communion.
Cell by infinitesimal cell,
You have replaced me.
Your Precious Blood
Now courses through my veins.
There should not be,
Much of me left.

If by chance
A stubborn core
Of "I" remains,

---

[47] Cellano, St. Thomas. *Biography of St. Francis,* see Appendix G.

[48] This word describes the action that takes place at the Catholic Mass when the bread and wine are transformed by the Holy Spirit into the Body and Blood of Jesus, as the priest prays the Words of Jesus from the Last Supper. Then we receive Him in Holy Communion so that He can transform us into Himself.

Let the Consecrating
Fire of Your Spirit,
Come upon me.
Then, like a log set ablaze,
Retains its form,
While it burns,
With heat and light,
Let my poor human form,
Flame out,
With the Beauty,
Of Your Presence.
Let me be a Living Flame
Of Your Love.
For there is not,
Much of me,
Left in this world.

ADORATION

I slip into our dimly lit church.
My heart skips a beat,
Surprised,
By the sense of Presence I feel.
It is palpable,
In the stillness.

In the candlelight of the altar,
I see a glimmer of gold. [49]
"He is here!"
My "Host"[50] welcomes me,
Into His Home,
Into His Presence.
The warmth of His love
Envelops me.

As I kneel in adoration,
My heart is silent before my God.
From His Heart,
Myriad streams of grace pour forth.
My soul leaps for joy,
As I hear His promise in my heart,
"I am with you always!"

"How is it, that so many,
Doubt Your Presence here, Lord?
How is it that the entire world is not clamoring,
For these doors

---

[49] The Consecrated Bread, the Eucharist, is placed in a Monstrance, a golden receptacle that resembles a sunburst, for Adoration of the Real Presence of Jesus.

[50] Host is the term we use to refer to the Consecrated Bread.

To be open day and night,
So that we can come,
And adore You, our God?

My adorable Jesus,
You are lifted up,
Here, on our altar.
In Your mercy,
With Your captivating Beauty,
And the Power of Your Love,
Draw everyone to Your Heart!"

DO NOT FEAR

We sang out gloriously,
At Midnight Mass,[51]
"Glory to God in the highest
And on earth peace to people of good will."

My mind wandered,
To those places in our world
Where men are fighting,
Women and children
Hiding, crying, and dying.
Only violence, suffering and ill will,
Can be found in their land.
"What does Christmas mean for them?"
I mused in my mind.
"Will peace ever come there?
What does Your angel say to them?
O God, let me hear Your Word."

"A Reading from the Holy Gospel according to Luke."
The Word intruded on my thoughts.
The priest proclaimed:
"Do not fear! I bring you tidings of great joy!"
My heart leapt within me!
"Do not fear!"
"Do not fear!"
The message became a mantra in my heart.
"Do not fear" world, you are loved,
"Do not fear" though your heart is torn,
"Do not fear" world,
Though darkness clouds your sight,
"Do not fear" though you are dying,

---

[51] Roman Catholic Liturgy traditionally celebrated at Midnight on Christmas
Eve, marking the hour Jesus may have been born.

"Do not fear!"
For a Savior came for you this night.
You will find Him wrapped in the swaddling clothes,
Of your own suffering.
In your darkness and pain
He gifts you,
With His peace,
He gifts you His Word,
"Do not fear!"[52]
Light has swallowed the night,
and death!

---

[52] *Luke 2:10-12.*

"Jesus went through all the towns and villages,
teaching in their synagogues,
proclaiming the good news of the kingdom and
healing every disease and sickness.
When he saw the crowds, he had compassion on them,
because they were harassed and helpless,
like sheep without a shepherd.
Then he said to his disciples, 'The harvest is plentiful,
but the workers are few.
Ask the Lord of the harvest, therefore, to send out
workers into his harvest field.'"
Matthew 9:35-38

THE SOWER

I needed someone to help,
My fields were ready for grain,
I went to the world and looked.
My choice fell upon you,
I called and you answered Me,
With willing heart and hands.

I gave you the seed of My Word,
I gave you the spade of My Love,
I showed you my Elder Son,
He taught you the manner of sowing,
On a hill with outstretched arms,
He showed the manner of loving.

Now walk to the top of that hill,
Now pass through the crossbar gateway,
Now work in the land to be sown.
I give you the Power of Christ,
I give you the souls, so precious,
Now work, till they are all My Own.

ORDAINED

For others,
They offered to God their lives,
Hands anointed,
For Holy Things.
Their hearts etched deep,
With the Image of CHRIST,
He gazes,
Through their eyes.

Despite all the years of sacrifice,
Humanity remains their home.
While, daily in prayer for all,
His mercy they appeal,
It is still their own weakness,
That they, so often, feel,

Yet, in all, whom they meet,
HIS LIFE within them
Works Its grace.
No matter,
Their clay feet,
It is His Light in them,
They see,
His Words, they hear,
His Love, they feel.

Bonded forever,
Are these men,
With God,
Priest and Victim,
Alter Christus.[53]

---

[53] Latin for 'Other Christ.'

"Wives, be subject to your husbands as you are to the Lord.
For the husband is the head of the wife,
just as Christ is the head of the Church...
Husbands, love your wives,
just as Christ loved the Church and gave himself up for her..."
Ephesians 5:22,23,25

ONE IN CHRIST

Trinity Mystery mirrored,
As center of one reaches out to know,
to touch,
to love,
Another.

Love flows from two,
Making two, one center,
one life,
one love,
A new Spirit born.

Spirit urging two toward evermore,
Becoming one, in giving love,
in giving self,
in giving life
To others.

A new love, a new life,
From "two made one"
that never was,
is now,
and will be,
Forever.

Celebrate Trinity!
Mystery of God etched out,
in human flesh,
in human hearts,
in man and woman
+Becoming Christ+

My Wedding Day, May 23, 1987

THE BLESSING CUP

*"The Blessing Cup is our Communion with
the Blood of Christ."*[54]

As you have shared your lives
For Fifty Years,
Drinking the wine of joy
And sorrow,
The wine of busy days
And restless nights,
The wine of love expressed,
And pain endured.

May you continue to share,
This Blessing Cup,
Drinking the wine,
The mingling of your lives
With the Life of Christ,
With the Blood of Christ.

Realize that He takes it all,
The moments of light and darkness,
Of sin and grace,
Of weakness and strength,
And transforms them into
Moments of Salvation.

Your story together,
Your history,
Of enduring faithful love,
In the face of suffering
And human weakness,

---

[54] Responsorial for Mass of the Lord's Supper, Holy Thursday in Roman
Missal.

Becomes His Story,
Revealing to the world
The Enduring Faithful Love of God.

Man and Woman made one in Marriage,
Celebrate in Human Flesh,
The Wedding Feast of the Lamb.

CHAPTER FIVE

Love 's Devotion

"Hear, O Israel, the LORD, our God, is LORD alone.
You shall love the LORD, your God,
with all your heart, and with all your soul,
and with all your might.
You shall keep these things that I command you
today in your heart."
Deuteronomy 6:4-6

Sacred Heart Altar, St. Bernard's Church, Mt. Lebanon, PA

*"While the Blessed Sacrament was exposed,
feeling wholly withdrawn
within myself by an extraordinary recollection
of all my senses and powers,
Jesus Christ, my sweet Master, presented Himself to me,
all resplendent with glory, His Five Wounds
shining like so many suns.
Flames issued from every part of His Sacred Humanity,
especially from His Adorable Breast,
which resembled an open furnace,
and disclosed to me His most loving and most amiable Heart,
which was the living source of these flames.
It was then that He made known to me the ineffable
marvels of His pure love and showed me to what an excess
He had loved men, from whom He received only
ingratitude and contempt."*[55]

---

[55] Private Revelations of the Sacred Heart of Jesus to St. Margaret Mary Alacoque, Dec. 27, 1673, 350 years ago.

"The principal thing is to stand before God
with the mind in the heart
and to go on standing before Him unceasingly
day and night until the end of life."[56]

AWAKE

I looked into my heart,
One day,
And Someone woke up.
Now she sits there,
Day and night,
Listening to secrets
And singing praises.
Whenever I peek,
I see her,
Attending
To the Divine Presence,
Her face lit,
With wondrous joy.
I try to stay awake with her,
But end up falling asleep,
In her arms.

---

[56] Definition of prayer by St. Theophan the Recluse from *The Art of Prayer:*
An Orthodox Anthology.

"This is how we know what love is:
he laid down his life for us,
and we in turn must be prepared
to lay down our lives for our brethren."
1 John 3:16

PROFESSION

"As a young man marries a virgin,
so will your builder marry you,
and as a bridegroom rejoices in his bride,
so will your God rejoice over you."[57]

Jesus, if I am to be Your Bride
I must suffer as did Thee,
Become a victim of Your love,
And be crucified for Thee.

Make my life, my cross, my Love,
Which I now embrace so lovingly,
Three nails that bind me close to it,
Obedience, poverty, chastity. [58]

May the Spear of Your Love,
Pierce deep my human heart,
And kindle there within,
Divine Love with one spark.

May a crown of thorns pierce through,
Make a flaming fire of that spark Divine,
Till my heart burns out with love,
And I fly to Thee, to be forever Thine.

---

[57] *Isaiah* 62:5

[58] Traditional Vows of those entering religious life in the Church and taken privately by individuals as a sign of commitment to God.

I became a Novice, Aug. 11, 1958

"This is My commandment, that you love one another
as I have loved you.
Greater love has no one than this, than to lay down
one's life for his friends."
John 15:12-13

THE CRY IS LOVE

Kneeling before an Image of Christ Crucified,
A piercing cry filled my soul,
The Wounds, the open Arms,
All called out,
"Love!"

It was too much for me,
I turned back to the rush of everyday life,
Keeping busy would help me forget,
That pleading, that cry!
Then I heard it, louder than before,
It seemed the whole world cried,
"Love!"

I looked around to see who was calling out,
An old woman looking through the trash,
The amputee with cup and pencils on the street,
Children playing in a vacant lot,
A delinquent just picked up by the police,
The drunk coming out of the bar,
A woman selling herself,
They all screamed at me,
They were pleading,
"Love!"

I tried to forget,
And picked up the morning paper,
This would distract me.
Isis Beheads Christians
20 Innocent Victims of Trafficking Found
Thousands Starve in the Sudan
Bomb Detonates a Church in Nigeria
Missing Child Is Found Dead
And then it pulsed madly through my soul again.
"Love!"

I could not stand the deafening cry,
Love!"
I screamed out at the world and God,
What can I do?
How can I stop this cry?"
The answer rushed like a torrent
Into my soul.
"Love,
Only love, will silence the plea."

And so, I too, must cry out now,
It is burning in my soul,
My plea to you,
My cry is,
"Love!"

IT COSTS SO LITTLE TO GIVE

Love is silent –
Love sometimes sleeps.
Why?
In ghettos, slums, war-torn countries,
Lonely faces ask, "Why?
Why must we meet hate?
Know injustice? Pain?
When love costs so little to give?"

Speak love –
Wake up sleeping hearts.
Turn and give yourselves to others.
A cheerful word – see the smile appear?
A seed of love is being planted.
A gentle touch,
A warm grip of the hand,
A smile,
It costs so little to give.

"Jesus said, 'Behold the Heart which has so loved men that it has spared nothing even to exhausting and consuming itself, in order to testify Its love; and in return, I receive from the greater part only ingratitude, by their irreverence and sacrilege, and by the coldness and contempt they have for Me in this Sacrament of Love.'" [59]

HEART OF JESUS

Heart of Jesus,
Burning furnace of charity,
First beating softly
In the Living Chalice,
Then slowly stopping,
On Calvary.

Heart of Peace,
Lasting comfort,
In which sorrows cease,
Compassionate at Cana, Naim, Bethany,
Forever loving
Where love is in need.

Heart of Agony,
Sorrow-filled,
Deep in Gethsemane,
Thorn-crowned, spear-pierced Heart,
Mocked by human malice,
Be adored and loved,
Through all eternity.

---

[59] Private Revelations of the Sacred Heart of Jesus to St. Margaret Mary Alacoque, June 16, 1975.

"Sacred Heart of Jesus, teach me perfect forgetfulness of myself, since that is the only way by which we can enter into You."
St. Claude de la Columbiere

MOLD ME

Claim my heart,
And all I have known,
Into a Heart
Just like Your own,
Mold me, Lord!

Just take this clay,
Of which I am made,
Into the Wound,
Within Your Side,
Press me, Lord,

Now, deep within,
Your Heart, I'll hide.
Now, deep within,
Let me abide,
Forever, Lord.

THE HOLY GRAIL

Jesus, Knights of old went in search of the Cup,
That held Your Precious Blood at the Supper.
Never finding it, the search goes on,
Not knowing 'what or where'
Of this Treasure.
Yet, You asked us,
"Can you drink of this Cup of which I drink?"
And then tell us, "You will indeed drink of it..."[60]

What is this Cup, this Holy Grail?
What vessel collected the Precious Blood,
Flowing from Your Body
In Gethsemane, in the scourging, in the crowning,
Veiling Your Holy Eyes and Face?
What is the goblet that received It
From Your Pierced Hands and Feet, streaming like fountains?
What Precious Cup was filled to the brim,
By the gushing forth from Your wounded Sacred Heart,
Pierced by a lance on Calvary?

This Cup, this Holy Grail is our earth, Lord Jesus.
Your Precious Blood
Drenched our world with Salvation.
The earth of which we are made,
Where we live our daily lives,
From which our daily bread, which nourishes us, grows,
Is our Cup, that I must indeed drink.

"I will take up the Cup of Salvation."[61]
It is the Vessel of my life.

---

[60] *Matthew 20:22-23.*

[61] *Psalm 116:13.*

Like You, Jesus, in Gethsemane,
I must say to the Father.
"Not my will but Thine be done." [62]
Yes, I will drink the Cup of my life,
With all its joys, sorrows, and losses,
With all its pain, boredom, and work,
Seeing in this Cup the Sweet Saving Nectar
Of Your Most Precious Blood,
With which You covered me on Calvary.
My life is my Holy Grail,
No need to search,
Just embrace.
Fiat!

---

[62] *Luke 22:42.*

"The heart is but a small vessel;
and yet dragons and lions are there,
and there poisonous creatures and
all the treasures of wickedness;
rough, uneven paths are there, and gaping chasms.
There likewise is God,
there are the angels,
the heavenly cities
and the treasures of grace;
all things are there."
St. Macarius

HOLY GOD

"Holy God!" [63]
I pray the words,
"Holy Mighty One!"
My heart trembles in Your Presence,
"Holy and Immortal One!"
In Your Light, I see my soul,
"Have mercy on me" a sinner,
I plead.

"Holy God!"
I cry!
"Holy Mighty One!"
Come and save me,
"Holy and Immortal One!"
Reach down and lift me up,
"Have mercy on me,"
Prostrate before You.

---

[63] he Trisagion Prayer: "Holy God, Holy Mighty One, Holy Immortal One" is
an ancient prayer in Christianity used in Eastern Liturgical Rites.

"Holy God!"
In my depths You reveal Yourself,
"Holy Mighty One!"
You are the
"Holy and Immortal One!"
Gazing with compassion on Your people,
"Have mercy on me,"
And draw me into Your Heart!

"Ever Holy and indivisible Trinity, I adore You profoundly,
I love You intensely and thank You perpetually.
For All and in the Hearts of all."[64]

MY TRIPTYCH

In wondrous silence, I kneel,
Before the Sacred Triptych[65] in my soul.

I

My Loving Father,
Embracing the Crucified Body of His Beloved Son,
Leans toward me,
Gathering me into that embrace.
"Come, Beloved Daughter,
See the One who died for thee.
Know, I have marked you as He."

II

My Risen Bridegroom,
Wounds all shining, gazes at me.
The radiance of His Eyes
Clothes me in a wedding garment of Light.
"Come within, beloved of My Heart, I know thee.
Your wounds are healed in Mine."

III

In the Luminous Wings of a Brooding Hen,
I see my home.
God's Spirit, as a loving Mother,
Nurtured me there all my life.
"Come, Beloved little One, rest under My Wings,
For I, LOVE, have nested in your heart."

---

[64] Piccarreta, Louisa, Servant of God. Book of Heaven, Vol. 4, 1/14/02.

[65] *A three-paneled devotional of Sacred Images.*

I know myself enfolded in a LOVE that created me,
died for me, nurtured me, called me,
crafted me, forgave me, healed me,
crucified me and wedded me as Its own!

"My adorable Jesus may our feet journey together.
May our hands gather in unity.
May our hearts beat in unison.
May our souls be in harmony.
May our thoughts be as one.
May our ears listen to the silence together.
May our glances profoundly
penetrate each other.
May our lips pray together to gain mercy from
the Eternal Father."[66]

---

[66] KIndlemann, Elizabeth. "Unity Prayer," p.25, *The Flame of Love*. Drexel Hill, PA: Children of the Father Foundation. 2015.

MY OTHER SELF

Will you take them to your heart?
Will you hold them there for Me?
Will you give them time to grow,
Into what I plan for them to be?

Will you carry now this burden?
I have carried My Cross, so long.
I know that you will help Me.
And I will make you strong.

Bring them daily to My altar.
We will feed them My Body and My Blood.
I will teach them to remember,
My Father's tender Love.

Bring them here for adoration.
My Love will penetrate their heart,
Removing sin and imperfections,
My grace to them impart.

Nourish them throughout the day,
With sacrifice, prayer, and love.
Slowly all of them will grow,
As they come to know Our Love.

Together, You and I,
We will save them from themselves,
They are My Beloved children,
Will you hold them in your heart,
My Other Self?

ALL IS MINE

Mine is the sun,
Dazzling our God with praise in the morning,
Mine is the moon,
Humbly bowing in adoration at night,
Mine is the mountain peak,
Piercing the clouds with thanksgiving,
Mine is the mighty ocean,
Beating the rhythm of God's Heart.

Mine is the elephant,
Trumpeting praises at dawn.
Mine is the roar of the lion,
Calling for mercy at twilight,
Mine is the coo of the dove,
Rejoicing in voicing its love,
Mine is the song of the thrush,
Singing Vespers at eventide.

Mine the lost lamb in the brambles,
Bleating its distress to God,
Mine is the mighty stallion,
Thundering praise across the plain,
Mine is the kitten trusting,
Snuggling close to momma.

Mine is the sweet canary,
Singing an 'alleluia' in its cage,

Mine is the baby's first cry,
At its aborning,
Mine the last sigh,
Of the holy dying of a monk,
Mine is the suffering,
Of every man and woman,
Mine is their joy,
As they come to know the Lord.

Mine is the world
And all of creation.
For I am its voice
Giving thanks to the Lord,
Forever exulting
Before the One who made us,
For all, with all and in all,
Worship and praise!
Mine is the sunset,
God's loving good night.

Sunset in the Winter Sky

GOING TO MORNING MASS

We are an early morning people,
Still shrouded in darkness,
Subject to night-time fears,
Even as hope rises in our hearts.

The setting of the moon
And the absent beauty of the stars,
Signal, the sun's first rays,
The coming of dawn!

Like butterflies with dew on our wings,
We wait patiently for His light and warmth,
To free us from our soul's slumber,
To take flight to God's Heart.

Cling to that hope,
Even if the darkness makes you stumble,
The Son's rising light will reveal,
His growth in you through the night.

Sun Call

Butterflies slumber
In stalky dew-speckled beds,
As morning sun
Peers through cobwebbed windows,
Teasing them awake.
In morning delight
They shake sandy dew from winged eyes,
And take yawning stretching flight
To sweet breakfast. [67]

---

[67] Written while sitting in a field watching the sun come up, and seeing the
butterflies awaken and fly away from where they spent the night, at the
tops of thick grasses.

"Behold, I am standing at the door, knocking.
If one of you hears my voice and opens the door,
I will come in and dine with that person and
that person with me."
Rev. 3:20

COMING HOME

When I turn to pray,
I feel like,
I am coming home.
I open a door,
To darkness,
And suddenly,
I am flooded
With warmth and light,
And the loving embrace of family.
The fire is crackling,
The table is set,
And as we sit,
The Three and I,
To share a meal,
We feast,
On Warm Bread,
Sweet Wine.
And Inebriating Love.

I WOULD DIE

I did not know how thirsty I was,
Until this morning,
When I drank deeply
Of Your Sweet Presence.

How adaptable I am,
Trudging along, dry, and parched,
Thinking I am nourished,
While my spirit withers within,

Too busy to stop,
And drink,
From the wellsprings of prayer,
The dust from the desert of my heart,
Clouds my vision.

Were it not for the underground spring,
Of the Spirit,
Buried deep within my being,
I would die.

PSALM OF A WINTER RETREAT

You filled my senses, made for You,
As I walked through Your winter world,
And my soul burst forth in praise and thanksgiving:
For misty early morning walks,
As deep darkness edged to dawning light, I praise You!
For cool crisp walks,
As bright sky of morning hurried the night away, I thank You!

For the Morning Star,
Leading pale blue day to eager dawning, I praise You!
For the sun's rising,
Scattering golden radiance upon the horizon, I thank You!

For a rainbow crystal window
In the winter sky, I praise You!
For icy air nipping at my cheeks and nose,
Challenging my coming, I thank You!

For snow — flaked, rolled, powdered, and dumped,
Drifting our world in soft whiteness, I praise You!
For the snow crunching under my feet,
As I walk these hills, I thank You!

For frozen wide river,
Fading into white sky, I praise You!
For the vast tundra-like wilderness,
Wild with cold, I thank You!

For the howling of a relentless North cold wind,
Covering the landscape with sheer sheen of ice, I praise You!
For the icing on the trees
Shining in the sun, I thank You!

For the cracking of ice on the slowly moving river,
Encroaching glacier-like upon the sandy beach, I thank You!
For the warm South wind breaking
The Midas-touch of winter's cold, with melting, I praise You!

For sun-sailing unimpeded on clear blue ocean sky,
Bringing warmth to winter weary world, I thank You!
For wooded earth's quiet warmth,
Rising through melting snows, I praise You!

For birds, shattering the silent woods' air,
Mounting to mighty exaltation for winter's thaw, I thank You!
For holly trees hinting at springtime
In the winter woods, I praise You!

For the sight of fleeting cardinals, sparrows, and blackbirds,
Rabbits, squirrels, and white-tailed deer, I thank You!
For the sounds of pecking and scampering,
Twittering, honking, and cawing, I praise You!

For pre-spring rain drops on branches,
Sparkling like jewels in the morning light, I thank You!
For an evening delight of black silhouetted trees
Against the sunset-colored skies, I praise You!

For the water shimmering silver
In a full moon rising, I thank You!
For seeing Your sun rise over the trees,
While Your moon sets over the river, I praise You!

For all that has delighted
My heart and my eyes, I thank You and praise You!
But none of this can compare nor can words describe,
The experience of Your Presence.

Your strong tender healing hand,
Touched all that I am, claiming me as Your own.
In the silence of these days my whole being has delighted,
In the overwhelming Love of God, my Savior!
I praise You! I thank You! I worship You, my God!

TORNADO WATCH

Holy!
Silver-streaked dark sky thundered out,
Then a raucous buzzer,
Sends unsuspecting holiday people
Whirling down passages to dead center shelter,
What a motley crew.

Holy!
Above us the embattled sky twisted, stabbed,
Creaked, roared, thundered, and groaned,
Battering the earth in fury,
Devouring anything
Resisting its claim to power.

Holy!
Crowded in our oblong nest, we see
A gallery of question-marked and answered faces,
Boredom, resistance, adventure, fascination, contentment.
'From the fullness of the heart the face speaks.'

Lord!
Nature 's Lord demands obedience,
That none dare withstand.
We wait and He gives quiet permission,
To resume our lives once more,
In the shadow of future demands.

God of Power and Might!
He has marked and claimed our hearts and spirits.
Gentle fascination leads us, daring ones,
In awe of His powerful Presence,
To break the bonds of steel structured world
And stand on the roof, naked hearted before the open sky.

Heaven and Earth are full of Your Glory!
The Mighty Glory breaks open the sky,
And cracks with light, in a thousand places,
The fragile shell of our security.
Uncontrollable, Holy, Awesome One!

Hosanna in the highest!
Uncontrollable, Holy, Awesome God,
Writes His Lightning Name in the sky,
Etching it on mind's eye never to be forgotten
"HOLY!"
Fascinated spirits would break further the ties to earth.

Blessed is He Who comes in the Name of the Lord!
The thunder mounts, announcing a coming.
What coming do rent heavens tell
As jagged lights engulf and crash,
Upon submissive earth and hearts?
With fluid power the earth is taken captive
And He comes in a Storm of Glory!
Hosanna in the Highest![68]

---

[68] "Holy, Holy, Holy" is a chant from Catholic Liturgy.

COME, LORD JESUS!

I have looked into my life, Lord,
and I know that I need You,
but where do I begin to seek You?
I have unfurled my heart's banner,
and rolled out the welcome mat,
or at least I have said a timid,
"Come, Lord Jesus."
But how do I recognize You,
amid the hustle and bustle
of this silver-bell time of the year?

Christmas shopping, carol singing, cookie baking,
window washing, corner scrubbing, attic hunting,
tree trimming, card writing, present wrapping,
Are You hidden somewhere,
in the middle of all of this, Lord?

Are You hidden in the loneliness
and sadness of hearts that ache,
because they are alone with no one to love,
because the one they love is no longer here,
because sickness shadows their days,
because they have no hope for joy or peace?
Are You hidden
in this pain somewhere?

Thank You, Lord,
for this time to stop,
for this time of peace and quiet.
Listen as I call to You.
Come, Lord, of my Christmas shopping,
help me pick each gift with love.

Come, Lord, of my card writing,
let my words speak Your Love.
Come, Lord, of my house cleaning,
help me make a place of love.
Come, Lord, of my busyness,
let me rest in Your Love.
Come, Lord, of my loneliness,
let it lead me to Your Love.
Come, Lord, of my sorrow,
let it be filled by Your Love.
Come, Lord, of my despair,
let me hope again in Your Love.

Come, Lord Jesus, to all of us,
Come today with Your Love,
You alone are our Savior,
You alone can heal hearts,
You alone have the power,
You alone are our God!

*"Behold, I have inscribed your name
on the palms of my hands;
your walls are continually before my eyes."
Isaiah 49:16*

PSALM OF LIFE

O God! How glorious is Your Name over all the earth,
How marvelous the works of your hands.
You are a God that gives life,
A God whose touch,
Can make a seed break into blossom.
Touch our lives, O God,
And bring fresh, springtime life to us.

Make our hearts glad to be in your Presence,
Glad to be alive.
Help us to find joy in all of life, today.
Help us to find your Image,
In the life of every person.
Make us a people that Loves life, all of Life!
As you protect our lives,
Make us guardians of life.
Show us how to give life to each person we meet.

Then we will
Cherish the beginnings of life,
Nourish the young life,
Protect the fragile life,
Strengthen the weak Life,
Find the lost life,
Respect the aging life,
Tend the wounded life,
And love the Source of life.

Give us grace to rise each morning,
and embrace life with a real love:
Feasting on its joys,
Drinking its sorrows,
Bearing its burdens,
But taking hold of its every moment,
Realizing that
You are in the midst of our life!

Help us never to be so caught up in making a living,
That we have no time to Live!
Lord of life, life giving God,
Thank You for the Gift of Life!

CHAPTER SIX

Human Love

We love because He first loved us.
Whoever claims to love God yet hates a brother or sister
is a liar.
For whoever does not love their brother and sister,
whom they have seen,
cannot love God, whom they have not seen.
And he has given us this command:
Anyone who loves God must also love their
brother and sister."
1 John 1:19-21

My mother's 80th Birthday with five of her seven children

"Love has no other desire but to fulfil itself.
But if you love and must needs have desires,
let these be your desires:
To melt and be like a running brook
that sings its melody to the night.
To know the pain of too much tenderness.
To be wounded by your own understanding of love;
And to bleed willingly and joyfully.
To wake at dawn with a winged heart
and give thanks for another day of loving;
To rest at the noon hour and meditate love's ecstasy;
To return home at eventide with gratitude;
And then to sleep with a prayer
for the beloved in your heart
and a song of praise upon your lips."[69]

---

[69] Gibran Kahlil. " On Love" from *The Prophet,* pp13-14. *New York:* Alfred A. Knopf, Inc. 1976.

"The man said,
'This one is bone of my bones and flesh of my flesh.
She shall be called woman
because she was taken from man.'
This is why a man leaves his father and his mother
and joins with a wife, and the two become one flesh."
Genesis 2:23-24

MY BELOVED

My beloved,
Like a strong willow tree,
Bows his branches,
Gracefully,
Lifting me high,
Enfolding me,
In his sheltering
Arms of love.

Here I am touched,
By sweet tenderness,
My longing heart,
Now all at rest,
This is the ending,
Of my quest,
Being now blest,
By God above.

We journeyed alone,
Far and wide,
Now we're together,
Side by side,
Now we're at home,
No need to hide,
Finding great joy,
We abide in His Love.

*"Anyone who loves me will obey my teaching.
My Father will love them, and we will come to them
and make our home with them."*
John 14:23

TABERNACLE OF FLESH

I will contemplate You now, Lord,
In this tabernacle of flesh,
I call my husband.
You have taken him,
As Your own Dwelling Place,
Saying, "This is My Body,"
You give me Eucharist,
In his love,
And challenge my faith,
In his weakness.
In him You bear the cross,
Of my weakness,
When my human frailties,
See only his,
And react.
In him You forgive me
And challenge me,
To forgive,
As he responds,
With Your Grace,
"I apologize."

He is my Way of Holiness.
Through him You surely lead me,
Deeper into the Mystery of Love,
The Mystery of dying to self,
The Mystery of union,
With Your all-pervading Presence.
I contemplate You, Lord,
In the tabernacle of Teofan.

FAMILY

Though planted now in separate places,
With other branches,
Wound tightly around our own,
Common roots of Mother love,
And Father strength,
Run deep in our lives.

Memories of childhood days,
Of joy and laughter,
Light up in our minds.
Our hearts are warmed by the bond of love,
That gave us birth, our faith,
And one another.

We bear the sign in our hearts and faces,
My sisters, my brothers,
Forever, we are family.
But one bond of love, gives birth to another,
And we have set our roots,
In families of our own.

Though others come into the circle of our lives,
And distance comes between us,
We know, though now apart,
Even in death, we are not alone.
In love we can always be,
'Home' for one another.

MOTHER

Love spills out from you,
Anyone near you
Gets it all over themself,
Joy is like your face.

Sweetness is your talk,
All your words are honey,
That sticks to hearts,
Gentle is your hand.

Kindness is wrapped round you,
When anyone meets you,
They get wrapped in it too.
You are beautiful.

You are a mother,
At dawn you love,
At noon you love, at dusk,
Your heart never sleeps.

Children, yours we are,
You let us eat you up,
You are delicious.
You give yourself.

You belong to us,
You are our Mommy,
Our mom, our mother.
We love you, Mom.

THE FAMILY QUILT

My old family quilt,
Is showing signs of wear,
Frayed edges, loose threads, little holes,
Where unwanted visitors have feasted.
I have three choices: discard it, let it be to unravel further,
Or take on the task of repair.

I chose to repair it.
It will take attention and time,
A slow restoration of family ties.
It means sending out,
Strengthening threads of love and care,
To draw stray edges back into the quilt.
Reaching out, to share memories, and journeys taken,
Will tighten up the loose threads,
And bring new brilliance to the fading colors.
Patches of forgiveness will need to be applied,
To repair those unwanted holes.
I can begin the process,
But the more that take part in it,
The more beautiful this old family quilt can be.
We are not alone in this world.
We come into it through a family,
We create families of our own,
And belong to God's family,
Ultimately destined to live,
As family in His Kingdom!
Those who first wove this quilt,
Are already there!

We can choose to exile ourselves,
And live on islands of our own making,
But then we will never experience,

The warmth, protection, and joy,
Of being wrapped in an old family quilt,
When the day is cold,
And the night is long and dark.

On this journey through our world,
Will you join in the work of restoration,
Of the old family quilt?

DESTINATION

Our encounter
With another,
Cannot be other,
Then marked with
The Cross
+
Though set on a trajectory >>>>
To the same destination
Each of us
W
a n
d
e
r s,
detours,
Losing our way and *focus.*

Our meetings
Become intersections X +
We + cross paths,
We are at odds \ /
Hopefully, in dialogue
With His Word and each other,
We can come to see @ @
That we have a common destiny *
Our hearts should be,
Set on ONE THING,
Not on our m e a n d e r I n g.

Lest we S curve out of control,
God feeds us.
One Bread, One Cup, One Word,
Leading us, someday,
To meet,
In His Heart.

WHAT DO YOU SAY

Lord, what do you say,
About this love of mine,
This heart that has opened,
To include another
So that I now, no longer,
Find me alone?

Lord, what do you say,
You, who first walked these hills,
And valleys of my soul,
Gently loving and calling forth
Life and love?

What do you say,
Lord, Who alone knows,
All the tears and pain,
The joys and growth,
This love has engendered,
You, Who are the source of love?

"I say,
Grow beautiful in love,
And strong through loving,
For you will always carry,
The joy and burden of another now.
You will learn in the mystery,
Of this sweet pain,
The meaning of My Love."

SOUL FRIEND

Soul friend,
Peace bringing presence,
Moments spent,
Sharing drops of life,
Varied colored,
Mixed rainbow moments,
Bringing gold,
In spiritual treasures,
Shared,
Entrusted,
Lovingly,
Kept Sacred.

HIS FRIENDS

Grace flows in meeting,
When one of Spirit greets another
And "deep calls to deep"[70]
Drawing Spirit forth together.

No time bars knowing,
When Spirit love is in encounter,
Opening depths within,
Revealing oneness at the center.

Words will soon carry,
Spirit of one into the other,
Being at home now,
In the peace of His loving Presence.

Parting will deepen.
The knowing of another's being,
Indwelling of Spirit.
Will share more than seeing, speaking.

Together in Him,
The presence of each other sharing,
Beyond time and space now,
Grace will strengthen friendship's caring.

---

[70] *Psalm 42:7.*

LIKE A DEER

I shared my secrets.
Now another holds them,
Hopefully, in his heart.
It leaves me feeling,
Open and vulnerable,
Like a deer,
That has stepped out
Into a clearing,
And is seen.
By the one,
Who watched,
And waited,
For her coming.

Deer on my backyard hillside

UNSPEAKABLE

I stumble around in my words,
Lifting one, then another,
All useless to say,
While reality in me stretches
To reach, to touch,
Your expectant spirit.

Even as I speak the words,
I am sure will convey,
They betray not, the meaning,
Silently slipping,
From my heart
Into yours.

You know,
Without knowing words,
In a oneness
Of understanding,
In a union of spirits,
Forged in the depths,
Of the Loving Heart of God.

FRIENDSHIP VERSES

Sunshine

Good morning, Sunshine friend!
You brighten my heart's day,
With rays of love and joy
As you rise warmly
In my mind's morning!
Have a beautiful day!

Sky

Blue Sky friend, I feel so free,
In your wide-open friendship!
You make my day a celebration,
Of unclouded joy,
And give me room to grow in boundless love.
I like being with you!

Wind

Free spirit, Wind friend!
Playfully catching my life in your movements,
Creating moments of silly laughter
As you upset
My boring routine!
You are such a joy to be with!

Flower

Flower friend, you petal my life with joy
As you blossom open,
Revealing inner secrets,
Sharing sweet nectar of your spirit within,
To nourish growing love and friendship!
You are beautiful!

Rose

Gentle love, Rose friend,
I touch you tenderly,
As one who knows, both your beauty and your pain,
You have brought to a heart, once closed,
A loving gentle presence.
Thank you for your love.

Tree

Strong silent friend of mine,
A sheltering Tree you have been for me,
Rooted firmly in your faithfulness,
You calm my anxious searching,
As I rest in your presence.
Thank you, my friend!

Water

Free flowing spirit friend,
Like Water tumbling into my life,
With the freshness of your presence
Bringing joy, life, and laughter
As you give your love freely.
Life means so much more to me now!

Mountain

I come to you, Mountain friend,
Strong and steady,
Beautiful and grand on the horizon of my life
You challenge me to greatness,
And fill my life with peace!
Thanks for always being there.

Star

Though you shine so deeply
In my thoughts, Star friend
I feel the pain of distance,
I long to see your full beauty,
And have you here with me.
I wish we could be together.

Moon

Moon friend, I sense a sorrow within you.
In the black silence that surrounds you,
Know that a sun shines,
In our friendship,
To warm and lighten you.
I keep vigil with you, my friend!

"I shall no longer call you servants,
because a servant does not know
what his master is doing.
I have called you friends
because I have revealed to you
everything that I have heard from my Father.
John 15:15

THE VASE

Waiting emptiness,
Like human heart,
That time, suffering
And wisdom
Has hollowed.
Happy to hold,
Flower moments of joy given,
Wine moments of love received,
Water moments of life shared.
Freely pouring out
To be empty again.
Always hopeful,
Waiting to hold again,
Precious passing moments,
Knowing that only Love Eternal
Can be held forever.

HIDDEN PRESENCE

Gentle friend of mine,
Silent light rose presence,
I want to find the words,
To say so much,
To capture elusive beauty
Of one so dear,
In poor unrhymed words
That say not enough.

I have watched the petals of you,
Open wide,
And glimpsed, the hidden center,
The Guest within.
Petals turning outward,
Always miss seeing,
Another only knows and tells,
Of Treasure there within.

For you, unknowing is enough,
And waiting,
And opening, yet wider still,
To reach the Other.
And as you open to love,
The Hidden One,
Is clearly seen, by all who look,
Upon the rose,

The silent light rose friend,
Now dying,
Petals falling freely,
Humbly showing,
Hidden gentle Presence.

YOU ARE MY FRIEND

Gentle friend,
Your reaching out,
Has called me forth,
To a fuller life and love.

Your warmth
And kindness,
Sheltered tender leaves,
Still fearing Son's light.

Learning to rejoice
In the giving of
Another's love,
Has made me strong.

Now in that strength
I dare risk,
The fullness of
Love's Light.

What can I give,
But the joy
Of knowing,
You are my friend!

YOU ARE THERE

I mused in the night,
Over images of you in my life,
They jousted for position,
Strange contrasts:
Steady rock,
Exhilarating drink,
Sheltering oak tree,
Scattering whirlwind,
Deep mountain lake,
Electric current,
Welcoming home,
Eager journey.

In my life,
Unmistakably,
You are there.
You are interesting!
You are my friend!
You are loved!

LITTLE LOVE POEMS

Knowing

A smile,
A touch,
A warm hello,
A few words
Shared in passing.

It doesn't take much,
For lives to touch,
For hearts to know
A friendship's caring.

Love's Moment

Joy is you,
Me with you,
Me as me
Because of you.

You love,
And I am me.
I love,
You.

Joy is love.
Joy is you.
Joy is me.
"Love me."
"I do."

Love's Wine

Given.
But never lost!
Kept,
While poured out.

What is left is more.
Then what is given.

Though gone,
Always here.
Long ago,
Yet, now gives life!

Other

I am woman!
He is man!
Always Other.

Creator's reminder,
Of our need,
For Another.

Be Careful

My heart stretches toward him.
Something has unfolded in me,
In the warmth of his smile.

Be careful, my heart!
Don't give,
Until the hand is open to receive,
Don't grasp,
For what is yet to be given.

Parting

Meeting,
And,
All too soon,
Parting.
Pain!
All too real!
Where does it come from?

Even Now

Lost love,
Lays bitter winter,
On the soul,
Icing over feelings.

Self stands stark,
Bleakly etched,
Against the dark sky,
Life's sap buried deeply.

But even now,
The purple crocus appears!

CHAPTER SEVEN

Love's Dark Night

He will sit refining and purifying;
he will purify the descendants of Levi
and refine them like gold or silver
so that they may in righteousness
offer due sacrifice to the LORD.
Malachi 3:3

"When love beckons to you, follow him,
Though his ways are hard and steep.
And when his wings enfold you yield to him,
Though the sword hidden among his
pinions may wound you.
And when he speaks to you believe in him,
Though his voice may shatter your dreams
as the north wind lays waste the garden.
For even as love crowns you so shall he crucify you.
Even as he is for your growth so is he for your pruning.
Even as he ascends to your height and
caresses your tenderest branches that quiver in the sun,
So shall he descend to your roots and
shake them in their clinging to the earth.
Like sheaves of corn he gathers you unto himself.
He threshes you to make you naked.
He sifts you to free you from your husks.
He grinds you to whiteness.
He kneads you until you are pliant;
And then he assigns you to his sacred fire,
that you may become sacred bread for
God's sacred feast.
All these things shall love do unto you
that you may know the secrets of your heart,
and in that knowledge become a
fragment of Life's heart."[71]

---

[71] Gibran, Kahlil. "On Love" from *The Prophet,* pp.11-12. New York: Alfred
A. Knopf, Inc. 1976.

UNINVITED

Death is not a polite guest,
Who calls ahead,
To let you know he is coming!
No, he is a brassy uninvited one,
Who invades without warning,
And leaves us quickly,
To pick up the pieces
Of our hearts and lives,
After he takes
That which we love best.

Jesus Weeps Over Jerusalem, painted by my husband

"We do not wish you to be uncertain, brethren,
about those who have fallen asleep.
You should not grieve as do those who have no hope."[72]

THE DEATH OF MY TEOFAN

Grief is real suffering.
The pain of separation
From one I love,
Sears my soul.

Questions haunt me,
unanswered,
Did he know
How deeply I loved him?
Was he afraid?
Where is he now?
Does he see me and my tears?

The pain of guilt pierces.
Why wasn't I more loving,
More patient,
More aware of his needs?
Why didn't I spend more time,
Painting with him in his studio,
Or do more
That would have pleased him,
Or made him happy?

Now I face,
This impenetrable wall,
Separating us.
This gray emptiness

---

[72] *1 Thess. 4:13.*

In which I see nothing,
Hear nothing and feel
Only pain!

"For You, Jesus, in reparation,
For the conversion of sinners."[73]

My only refuge is prayer.
A daily offering of this pain,
And of the gift that he was,
Giving him back to God.
In daily Communion
I pray for healing,
For each day
Of our life together.

Gradually,
Peace and light return,
Like the coming of dawn
In my darkness.
Until one day, as I envisioned,
The vast wall of death,
I see an opening,
Shaped like the Tomb
On Easter Morning.
The brilliance of His Resurrection
Breaks through this wall.
Jesus has conquered death.
It is not an end.
There is a way through.
I am not closed off
From the one I love.
He is just beyond that opening,

---

[73] A prayer to offer- up sufferings from the Apparitions of Our Lady of Fatima, see Appendix H.

Shining with the brightness
Of the Transfiguration,
Radiating joy,
That seeps into my heart.
Even now I know,
The joy he now knows.

Questions, doubts, guilts fade away,
In this certainty of his new life in God,
He knows and understands,
And loves me![74]

"Those whom we love and lose
Are no longer where they were before.
They are now wherever we are."[75]

---

[74] *See Appendix I, Poem written by my husband.*

[75] *St. John Chrysostom.*

AT HOME

Be not afraid, my loved ones,
I have gone before you,
Following the One who called so insistently, so lovingly,
And now I am here, I am at home!

I cannot tell you the fullness of the joy, life, and love,
That is mine now!
That goes beyond my speaking and your understanding.
But I want to say thank you for helping me on my
journey home,
For being with me, especially in the pain.
I now know the full meaning of that pain,
Which is still yours to carry,
And I say trust it and hold it as a mystery of love.

Be assured,
I have found that not one moment,
Of our real life together, has been lost.
It is all held in the Heart of Him who is our Life.
All the moments are here, and we are here together.
When you look for me, come to Him.

Be assured,
I love you with a love,
I could not even carry in my heart before,
For I now love you with the Heart of Him, Who is Love.
My love will continue to forgive and heal,
Strengthen and nourish your hearts.

Be assured,
I now know the full meaning of all that life holds,
The pain, as well as, the joy,

The confusion and weakness, as well as,
the certainty and strength,
For I now see it in His Eyes.

How much more .... I can be for you now,
As I intercede before the Face of Our Father for you.
I hold each of you in the embrace of the One who holds me!
And though you weep and are sad,
You will come to know that I am near,
and your hearts will rejoice.
'Life has not ended but merely changed,'[76]
For me and for you, whom I love.
Alleluia!

---

[76] From the Preface of the Funeral Liturgy of the Roman Catholic Church.

I SIT

I sit,
The sit of the weak.

My feet won't feel,
The grass between my toes.
No pounding on the track,
No rush, as I cut away the miles
In a distance run.
No ache of muscle as I strain
To lift my body up the sheer wall.
No panting breath as I reach
The top, and view the vista,
Beyond the hill.

I sit,
The sit of the weak.

In prayer,
My spirit seeks the Lord,
And with the closing of my eyes,
My mind delights,
In the horizon of the universe.
I climb the stairs of the Milky Way
And leap from planet to planet.
My body knows no limits,
No ache of muscle,
As I soar beyond the stars and galaxies,

And dance to the music of the spheres,
Praising God for His vast creation.

I sit.
The sit of the weak
But in Him, my spirit leaps for joy.

"The Lord is my Shepherd, there is nothing I shall lack.
He makes me lie down in green pastures;
he leads me to tranquil streams.
He restores my soul."
Psalm 23:1-3

DETERMINED SHEPHERD

Pain, my determined Shepherd,
Herds me to the heights,
Spying the waters
That will satisfy my burning thirst.
Sure, of the food
To nourish His Life within me.

I stay close to my Shepherd.
Though His staff can easily prod,
His touch
Is my security.
His watchful eye
Will never let me stray.

When in panic
I run from His rod,
And find myself lost in the brambles,
Suffering, His dog,
Seeks me out,
And drives me back to His side.

Pain, my determined Shepherd,
Herds me to the heights.

"Then he said to all who were with him,
'Anyone who wishes to follow me must deny himself,
take up his cross daily and follow me.
For whoever wishes to save his life will lose it,
but whoever loses his life for my sake will save it.'"
Luke 9:23-24

MY SELF

I thought,
She had died,
But she came,
Limping toward me,
My wounded self.
Tenderly,
I lifted her,
And took her,
To the Good Shepherd.
He carefully laid her
On His shoulders,
He bathed her wounds,
With His healing
Precious Blood,
He Held her close,
Until she died,
Then buried her,
Deep in His Heart.

And He has said to me, "My grace is sufficient for you,
for power is perfected in weakness."
Most gladly, therefore, I will rather boast about my weaknesses,
so that the power of Christ may dwell in me.
2 Cor. 12:3

PROTEST

Life is beautiful,
Each moment holds joy gift,
Offered freely.
Yet, here I stand,
At times, unable to receive,
Prisoner of life's past moments,
Not so gifted.

Fear holds back my free response,
To a moment's beauty.
Fear colors words and gestures,
Disappointments,
And all too human, forgettings,
With its ugly colors.

Fear holds me back,
From sharing self in joy,
She says:
"Be careful, be cautious,
You are not good enough,
You are not lovely,
You will surely do and say,
The wrong thing!"

Who will free me,
From this relentless jailer,
This forbidding presence,
Robbing me of joy,
And of being me with you?

"I do not understand my own actions.
For I do not do what I want; rather, I do what I hate….
I have the desire to do what is good,
but I cannot do what is good.
For I do not do the good I desire;
rather, it is the evil I do not desire that I end up doing.
Now if I do what I do not desire,
it is no longer I who do it, but sin that dwells in me.
I have thus discovered this principle:
when I want to do what is good, evil lies close at hand.
In my innermost self, I delight in the Law of God,
but I perceive in the members of my body another law
at war with the Law that I cherish in my mind.
Thus, I am made captive to the law of sin
that dwells in my members.
What a wretched man I am!
Who will rescue me from this body destined for death?"
Romans 7:15,19,22-24

BOUND

Fallen!
All is quiet now.
Moment of turbulence,
Temptation,
Gone now.

Did it really happen?
Or did bad dream,
Etch too clear!
On mind's eye?

Not willing, yet doing,
Not wanting yet taking.
No prayer comes before,
Yet after, tears.

Why weakness?
No wishing
Will remove.
No willing
Will prevent!

CUT OFF

Cut off from my center,
My source and daily sustenance,
My life became a desert,
Parched and empty
Longing for Living Waters.
How long can I go on?
How deep are my roots?
Will they reach the wellsprings,
Buried in my soul?
How long can I endure the exile,
The drought of my neglect
Of prayer.

Most cannot tell,
All seems well to them.
Except those who are close,
Feel the heat,
And wonder,
Where has her joy,
And strength,
And life gone?

Desert of Death Valley, CA

EXCAVATIONS

I cannot catch You!
Only the inner crumbling
Marks Your Presence.
You
b
o
r
e

d
e
e
p
Into my pinning,
Like some fire weevil,
Like some holy termite,
You gnaw away at my inner being,
Leaving a yawning

G
a   e
p   l
i   o
n g   h

An aching emptiness!
Excavator of my heart
Your coming is my undoing!
Let me catch You,
Or hurry, move in,
And be finished with me.

"Indeed, the Word of God is living and active.
Sharper than any two-edged sword, it pierces to the point
where it divides soul and spirit, joints and marrow;
it judges the thoughts and the intentions of the heart."
Hebrew 4:12

THE WOUNDING

Unguarded
Before the poised power
Of Your bow,
I tremble,
Wild Word of God,
Vulnerable to Your wounding.

Your flashing glance pierces,
Rooting me,
Like an ancient tree,
In my tracks.
Splitting and cleaving,
Leaving
My heart naked
To Your shaft.

Though fearing Your thrust,
I cry: "Be swift,
With Your arrowed missive,
And claim, in pain,
Your prey!"

The crucible is for silver and the furnace is for gold,
but it is the LORD who tests the heart.
Proverbs 17:3

NO REMAINS

Stealthily You crept in,
Pulling the cotter pin,
Crumbling the self
I thought I was.
Who are You,
That turns my cardboard castle to ash,
With Your Word,
Your touch, Your glance?
Rubble is all you leave behind,
And for what?
Frantically I sift through,
Trying to find
A piece here, there,
Anything,
To restore some semblance
Of what I know.
But nothing – no thing!
You are thorough,
Destroyer of images!

"Let nothing disturb thee, let nothing frighten thee,
All things are passing, God never changes.
Patient endurance, attains to all things,
Whom God possesses, in nothing is wanting,
Alone God is sufficient."
St. Teresa's Bookmark[77]

WAITING

I closed,
My heart.
Locked now.
In dark safety,
Alone,
Weeping,
I wait,
For the Other
To break in.

---

[77] Found in St. Teresa of Avila's Prayer Book

"He said, 'Go out and stand on the mountain before the Lord,
for the Lord will pass by.'
There was a powerful, strong wind that tore the mountain apart,
and shattered rocks before the Lord,
but the Lord was not in the wind.
After the wind, there was an earthquake,
but the Lord was not in the earthquake.
After the earthquake, there was a fire,
but the Lord was not in the fire.
After the fire, there was a tiny whisper.
When Elijah heard it, he wrapped his face in his mantle,
and went out and stood at the entrance to the cave.
The voice said to him, "What are you doing here, Elijah?"
1Kings 19:11-13

PHOENIX

My steps echo back to me,
As I walk the wasteland
Of what was once my security.
Strange voices rise up,
To taunt my emptiness,
My despair.

Haunting laughter
Mocks my pain, sears my soul,
Crushes the last vestige,
Of my pride,
Leaving only darkness.

But wait,
A faint whispering Sound,
Rises like a thread of Light,
A Phoenix, from my ruins.
"You are Mine."

FIND ME

You,
Mysterious One,
Who stirred my depths,
Excavated my heart,
Pierced through my defenses,
Crumbled my cardboard castle,
Turned all I thought I was to ash,
You,
Who called me,
On a journey
Deep and mysterious,
Filled me with love and desire,
So expansive,
Opened before me
A horizon
Vast and unknown,
You,
Find me!

SOUL-MAKING

Off to the mixer, self,
It is soul-making day.
The soul-chef waits,
Ready to stir the contents,
In the depths of my heart.
His words,
Like sure strokes of a spatula,
Bring to the surface,
Memories that had settled,
Breaking up the lumps of what
Was not well mixed,
Readying my soul for the heat.

EXPOSED

I shuddered with shame,
As your words and mine,
Like scalpels,
Cut through the scars,
Skillfully laying bare,
Unconscious fears and defenses.

You were not to see!
It was from you,
They were to be hidden,
Silent weapons.
How can I look into your eyes now,
Knowing, you know?

Yet there you sit,
Waiting to welcome
Whatever my SELF has, to give.

GOLD

Shame,
Like fuller's lye,
Like refiner's heat,
If only I can stand
The burning -
Gold!

UNSETTLED

Something has stirred,
Deep within me,
And waters once still
Now whirl,
With murkiness.
I can't take hold
Of any thoughts,
They all elude me.
Feelings and words
Jostling in my mind,
Images swirling,
Churning,
And leaving me
Unsettled,
In my depths.

INSISTENCE

The still small Voice,
Whispers within,
Delicate, gentle,
Easily missed,
In the clatter and din
Of everyday life.

Without that Voice
My soul would wither,
Like parched land
Without water,
Longing for
Living streams,
Deep within.

Then why do I
Run from it?
Hide from it?
Silence it?
Why do I struggle,
Against the peace of it?

Surrender, my soul,
Let down
Your resistance.
Open up, heart,
The Voice
Is insistent!

SOULQUAKE

Fired by the mighty Spirit of God,
A force from deep within
Has shaken me to my core.
My whole being trembles,
As if struck by a powerful earthquake.
Whole portions of my foundations are shifting,
Along the fault lines of my soul,
In the inner landscape of my being.

A sense of foreboding fills me.
What will be lost as I come apart?
What will rise up to take its place?
What will the new landscape of my soul look like?
Will the tremors ever stop?
Will I survive the aftershocks?
Lord, Jesus Christ, I cling to Your Name,
Have mercy on me a sinner!

RISEN

From the split,
In the bedrock of my soul
An Image rises,
A Figure comes forth,
A Wounded Warrior,
Like the Son of God,
Rising from my soul.
"You are Mine."

THE QUEST

I am on a quest
Will I find what I seek?
The journey is hard,
It is long and inward,
No map to follow,
No stars lead me on,
Only the night,
The black night,
The dark night!

Though the sun hurts my eyes
I cannot see light,
Only the darkness guides my quest,
In the blinding brilliance
I call out for help,
A Hand reaches out.
I cannot grasp it,
Unless I move on,
Into the Night,
The black Night,
The dark Night!

The blackness seeps into my soul,
Though fearing the darkness,
I cannot turn back.
I cannot see!
Where is the Hand?
Only the NIGHT
Holds me fast,
The black NIGHT
The dark NIGHT

I am on a quest,
Will I find what I seek?
There is no Hand to guide me,
I am in the NIGHT!
It crushes my being,
Takes hold of my soul,
I am forced to surrender,
To this terrible NIGHT
This awe-filled NIGHT
This HOLY NIGHT.

Suddenly,
The NIGHT is peace!
Soothing and gentle
It caresses me.
It begins to shimmer,
And shine like black silk!
And the NIGHT
Became as Bright as Day![78]
The HAND!
It holds me now!

---

[78] *Paraphrased Psalm 139:12.*

*"I am confident of this: that the one who began a good
work in you
will bring it to completion on the day of Christ Jesus.
It is only right for me to feel this way toward you,
because I hold you in my heart,"
Philippians 1:6*

EVERYTHING IS NOW

I asked God one day, "Is it lost?"
My willingness to let go,
As a child,
Of so much of this world,
To welcome You more fully in my life?

Those childhood offerings of candy,
Made sacred during Lent,
When I made the Stations on my knees,[79]
Those touches of a young girl's heart
Calling her to be Yours.
That youthful home-leaving and
Offering of my life, future home,
Husband and children,
Made holy in vows not fully understanding.
Those dreams of taking
The Word of Your Love to Africa,
And ending up teaching in Dearborn.
The unrelenting seeking,
To know You ever more deeply,
And the desire to be faithful,
In the face of my own weakness.

---

[79] Practices during the Lenten season in Catholic Church, see the Appendix J.

"Are they lost?"
Those many hours,
For many years,
I spent in prayer,
And knew,
Your Divine Presence so near?

"Was it real?"
When in a dream You grasped my hand
And said, "Don't worry."
When a nighttime voice proclaimed
"The Kingdom of God is within you."
When grasped by Light,
You said, "You are Mine."

Was it real?
When in prayer,
You took my heart
And gave me Your Own;
When Mary shared Her heart,
As she told me tales,
Only she could know;
When in my meditation,
You washed my feet,
Then tended my wounds,
And I tended Yours;
When Your Spirit drew me
Deep into Your Side,
To sit at table with the Three
And know Divine intimacy?

So many moments
Interspersed these mountain tops,

When I was far from my 'first love,'[80]
When I went my own way,
When I took back the offerings I had made,
When the darkness overtook the light,
And self and sin took hold of my heart,
And I wrestled with the mystery of sin and grace.

Suddenly, God was there,
And I heard Him say,
"Everything is now!
I see you as you were,
Are now,
And will be forever in My Eyes.
Nothing you can imagine,
Comes close to the desires I have for you,
And the reality of My Life within you.
The Self I see in you,
Is the Self I have created you to be.
Come, rest in my Heart."

---

[80] Rev. 2:4:"However, I have this complaint against you: you have lost the love you had at first."

"...behold, the kingdom of God is within you."
Luke 17:21 KJV

WE ARE NOTHING, GOD IS ALL

*"However, we hold this treasure in earthen vessels,
so that it may be clear that this immense power,
belongs to God and does not derive from us.
We are afflicted on all sides but not crushed,
bewildered but not sunk in despair,
persecuted but not abandoned,
struck down but not destroyed.
We always carry around in our body the death of Jesus,
so that the life of Jesus may also be manifested in our body.
For in our lives, we are constantly being
given up to death for Jesus' sake,
so that the life of Jesus may be revealed in our mortal flesh.
As a result, death is at work in us, but life in you.
Therefore, since we have that spirit of faith
about which it has been written:
'I believed, and therefore I spoke,'
we also believe, and therefore speak.
For we know that the one who raised the Lord Jesus
will raise us also with Jesus
and bring us side by side with you into his presence.
Therefore, we do not lose heart.
Even though our outer self is continuing to decay,
our inner self is being renewed day by day.
Our temporary light afflictions are preparing for us
an incomparable weight of eternal glory,
for our eyes are fixed not on what is seen
but rather on that which cannot be seen.
What is visible is transitory; what is invisible is eternal."*
2 Corinthians 9:7-18

"In the twilight of life,
God will not judge us
on our earthly possessions
and human successes,
but on how well we have loved."

St. John of the Cross

Sunset over Puerto Rico

ANNOTATED BIBLIOGRAPHY

Below is a list of spiritual writings that have
influenced my spiritual life.

St. Augustine of Hippo. *Confessions,* New York: Image. 1960.

Baltimore Catechism, Third Council of Baltimore, North
Carolina: TAN Books. 2010.
> Book used to teach the Catholic Faith from 1884
> until the 1970's based on St. Robert Bellarmine's
> Catechism. It has various levels and uses ques-
> tions and answers to elucidate faith.

Brother Lawrence. *Practice of the Presence of God*. Ada, MI:
Baker Books. 1989.
> In the 1600's, Brother Lawrence after spending
> time in the army, entered The Carmelite Order
> as a lay brother in Lorraine, France. He sought
> his way of holiness by attempting to remember
> God's Presence in whatever he was doing, praying
> the psalms, cooking the potatoes, sweeping,
> talking with people at the door. He walked with
> his heavenly Father in every moment of his life
> and achieved real peace of heart. After his death
> they discovered letters which he wrote to others
> in which he explained his method.

Cassuade, Jean Pierre De. *Abandonment to Divine Providence*.
Houston TX: Wellsprings, 2017.
> Holiness is achieved by abandoning yourself to
> God's Will in all events of life. Each moment and

what it brings, and all the duties of our ordinary life, if accepted, will unite us to God. God in turn will provide, for those who trust Him, all that they need to attain holiness, even the book you need to read or a person you need to meet for your spiritual growth. He speaks of the Sacrament of the Present Moment; God comes to you in whatever the moment brings. Jean Pierre De Cassuade was a Jesuit chaplain for the Visitation Sisters in Nancy, France in the 17th century, and wrote this treatise for their spiritual guidance.

Funk, O.S.B. Mary Margaret. *Tools Matter for Practicing the Spiritual Life*. New York: Continuum Press. 2001.

St. John of the Cross, *Collected Works of.* Washington, DC: ICS Publications, 1991.

Gibran, Kahlil. *The Prophet*. New York: Alfred A. Knopf, Inc. 1976. Kahlil Gibran was a Lebanese American writer, poet, visual artist, and philosopher. His parents were Maronite Christians, but his religious leanings were more diverse. He was born in Lebanon in 1883, then his family moved to Boston. He died in 1931.

Kindlemann, Ven. Elizabeth. *The Flame of Love*. Drexel Hill PA: Children of the Father Foundation. 2015. The diary of Ven. Elizabeth Kindlemann recounting private revelations of Jesus and Mary to this widowed mother in Hungary beginning in 1961. She was called to spread the message of the Flame of Love, allowing Mary to enkindle your heart with the Love of Jesus.

Loyola, St. Ignatius. *Spiritual Exercise of St. Ignatius*. North Carolina: Tan Books. 1999.

St. Margaret Mary, Autobiography of. North Carolina: TAN Books. 1986.

> Saint Margaret Mary was a member of the Visitation Order in Paray-Le-Monial in France in the 16th century. From her childhood God was drawing her into a relationship with Himself and directing her steps toward entering this convent. In her twenties she entered the convent and began experiencing extraordinary visions. Jesus appeared to her and showed her His Heart and asked that adoration and reparation be directed toward His Presence in the Holy Eucharist. He wanted her to make His desires known, that His Heart be displayed and honored. Her spiritual director, Saint Claude de Columbiere received these messages from her and was instrumental in spreading devotion to the Sacred Heart of Jesus. It is one of the great devotions in the Church to this day and a great Basilica was built in the Lord's honor, Sacre Couer in Paris.

Norwich, Juliana. *Revelations of Divine Love*. New York: Image. 1977.

Piccarreta, Louisa, Servant of God. *The Book of Heaven,* 36 Volume Journal. Canonsburg, PA: Blanc Pub.

> This is a journal of private revelations by Jesus to Louisa spanning 1899 to 1939, on the coming reign of the Divine Will. The volumes present the doctrine and method of living in the Divine Will and invite everyone to ask for and open themselves to receive this Gift from God. We've

been praying "Thy Kingdom come and Thy Will be done" for centuries. Now God wants to bring that about. These volumes should be read under the guidance of a priest who has studied them. Father Celso and Father Ianuzzi are two priests whose teachings you can find on the YouTube channel. All the volumes of the Book of Heaven can be read, listened to, or downloaded for free on various websites, such as, Queen of the Divine Will.

Roman Missal, 3rd Edition. Washington DC: USCCB. 2011.

Stevens, Rev. Clifford. *One Year Book of Saints.* Huntington, IN: Sunday Visitor Books. 1989.

St. Tersea of Avila, *Collected Works of. Washington, DC:* ICS Publications, 1980.
> St. Teresa of Avila was a Carmelite nun in the 1500's who had mystical experiences in her early forties that led to her deep conversion to Christ. She became a great teacher of prayer and the spiritual life and along with St. john of the Cross reformed the Carmelite Order that had strayed from its ideals. She wrote her autobiography as a witness to conversion and her classic, *The Interior Castle,* on growth of a soul in prayer.

St. Therese of Lisieux. *The Story of a Soul, Autobiography.* North Carolina: TAN Books. 2010.

The Way of the Pilgrim. Boulder, CO: Shambala Classic. 2001.

APPENDIX A

ST. IGNATIUS LOYOLA AND PRAYER "ANIMA CHRISTI"

Anima Christi [81]

Soul of Christ, sanctify me.
Body of Christ, save me.
Blood of Christ, inebriate me.
Water from the side of Christ, wash me.
Passion of Christ, strengthen me.
O Good Jesus, hear me.
Within Your wounds hide me.
Permit me not to be separated from Thee.
From the wicked foe, defend me.
At the hour of my death, call me
And bid me come to Thee,
That with your Saints,
I may praise Thee,
Forever and ever. Amen

This prayer is attributed to St. Ignatius of Loyola.

A SPANISH NOBLEMAN soldier from the 16th century, St. Ignatius of Loyola's long recovery from a leg wound sustained in battle led to his conversion from soldier to saint. Resolving to follow no earthly king, he chose to follow Christ the King in the battle against evil in himself and the world. He chose Mary as his Lady and pledged his fidelity to her. In his religious classic, *Spiritual Exercises*, he presents meditations that lead you from a contemplation of God's Love and reflections on sin,

---

[81] Latin for Soul of Christ.

to a conversion of living under Christ's banner and following
Him to the Cross for the greater glory of God. He founded the
Jesuit Order.

APPENDIX B

JULIANA OF NORWICH

JULIANA OF NORWICH was an English Mystic who dedicated her life to prayer while living in a small enclosure attached to the Church of St, Julian in Norwich, England. Taken care of by a servant, she was provided with food and the necessities of life. At some point during these years, she became quite ill and was close to death. After the priest anointed her, instead of death, she received sixteen revelations from Our Lord Jesus regarding His love for us which became the focus of her book, *Revelations of Divine Love*. These revelations occurred in 1373, 650 years ago.

In chapter 24 she writes:

"Then with a happy face our Lord looked at his wounded side and gazed into it rejoicing. With his sweet gazing he drew forth the understanding of his creature through that same wound into his side within. And then he showed a fair delectable place large enough for all of mankind who shall be saved to rest there in peace and love. With this he brought to my mind his most valuable blood and the precious water which he let pour out completely for love.

With this sweet vision he showed his blissful heart cut even in two, and with the sweet rejoicing he showed my understanding, the blessed Godhead, in part, stirring the poor soul to understand It, as it may be put into words—that is, to comprehend the endless love that was without beginning, is, and ever shall be. With this our good Lord said most blissfully, 'See how I loved you!' It was as if he said, 'My darling, behold and see your Lord, your God, who is your Maker and your endless joy! See what delight and endless bliss I have in your salvation. For my love, enjoy it now with me.'"

APPENDIX C

POEMS OF ST. JOHN OF THE CROSS

ST. JOHN OF the Cross, a Spanish priest, mystic, poet, and spiritual writer from the 1500's is considered a master of spiritual life and is a Doctor of the Church. He and Saint Teresa of Avila, two of the greatest teachers on prayer, cooperated in reforming the Carmelite Order that had become lax in the practices of the spiritual life. Spending decades in contemplative prayer, he authored books about his experiences and expressed them in his poems. He is recognized as one of the foremost Spanish poets.

Living Flame of Love

O living flame of love
that tenderly wounds my soul
in its deepest center!

Since now you are not oppressive,
now consummate! if it be your will:
Tear through the veil of this sweet encounter!

O sweet cautery, O delightful wound!
O gentle hand! O delicate touch
that tastes of eternal life
and pays every debt!
In killing you changed death to life.

O lamps of fire!
in whose splendors the deep caverns of feeling,
once obscure and blind,

now give forth, so rarely, so exquisitely,
both warmth and light to their Beloved.

How gently and lovingly
you wake in my heart,
where in secret you dwell alone;
and in your sweet breathing,
filled with good and glory,
how tenderly you swell my heart with love.

Advent Poem

"If you want, the Virgin will come walking down the road
pregnant with the Holy and say, 'I need shelter for the night.
Please take me inside your heart, my time is so close.'
Then, under the roof of your soul,
you will witness the sublime intimacy,
the divine, the Christ, taking birth forever,
as she grasps your hand for help,
for each of us is the midwife of God, each of us.
Yes, there, under the dome of your being,
does creation come into existence eternally,
through your womb, dear pilgrim,
the sacred womb of your soul,
as God grasps our arms for help:
for each of us is His beloved servant never far.
If you want, the virgin will come walking down the street,
pregnant with Light, and sing!"

APPENDIX D

FAVORITE PSALMS

Psalm 139

1 You have searched me, LORD,
   and you know me.
2 You know when I sit and when I rise;
   you perceive my thoughts from afar.
3 You discern my going out and my lying down;
   you are familiar with all my ways.
4 Before a word is on my tongue
   you, LORD, know it completely.
5 You hem me in behind and before,
   and you lay your hand upon me.
6 Such knowledge is too wonderful for me,
   too lofty for me to attain.
7 Where can I go from your Spirit?
   Where can I flee from your presence?
8 If I go up to the heavens, you are there;
   if I make my bed in the depths, you are there.
9 If I rise on the wings of the dawn,
   if I settle on the far side of the sea,
10 even there your hand will guide me,
   your right hand will hold me fast.
11 If I say, "Surely the darkness will hide me
   and the light become night around me,"
12 even the darkness will not be dark to you;
   the night will shine like the day,
   for darkness is as light to you.
13 For you created my inmost being;

you knit me together in my mother's womb.
¹⁴ I praise you because I am fearfully and wonderfully made;
your works are wonderful,
I know that full well.
¹⁵ My frame was not hidden from you
when I was made in the secret place,
when I was woven together in the depths of the earth.
¹⁶ Your eyes saw my unformed body;
all the days ordained for me were written in your book
before one of them came to be.
¹⁷ How precious to me are your thoughts,[a] God!
How vast is the sum of them!
¹⁸ Were I to count them,
they would outnumber the grains of sand—
when I awake, I am still with you.
²³ Search me, God, and know my heart;
test me and know my anxious thoughts.
²⁴ See if there is any offensive way in me,
and lead me in the way everlasting.

Psalm 131
¹ A song of ascents. Of David.
O Lord, my heart[b] is not proud, nor are my eyes raised too high.
I do not concern myself with great affairs
or with things too sublime for me.
² Rather, I have stilled and calmed my soul,[c]
hushed it like a weaned child.
Like a weaned child held in its mother's arms,
so is my soul within me.
³ O Israel, put your hope in the Lord
both now and forevermore.[d]

APPENDIX E

SAINTS MENTIONED IN POEMS AND QUOTES

First a Word About Saints

THE CHURCH DOES not make saints but merely recognizes what God's grace has done. The Church facilitates this action of grace by providing us with the Sacraments and teaching on prayer and virtuous living. When a holy person dies, the evidence of the person's life leads the Church to study their life and writings, making sure they lived a life of heroic virtue which held true to the teachings of Christ and His Church. At that point they are called Servant of God. When saintliness is determined by this study, they are called Venerable and then the Church waits for God to show His approval. Members of the faithful will pray that the holy person intercede with God for them in difficult situations, usually ones of sickness. It is not until a miracle of physical healing occurs, which is beyond a doubt through the holy person's intervention, that the person is declared Blessed. Then the church waits again for a second miracle, before declaring them a Saint. Martyrs are the exception, because of the heroic willingness to give their life for Christ, there is no question of their holiness.

There are an untold number of holy people in heaven who are saints that we know nothing about. Why does God want particular holy people to be declared saints? He raises up certain people to give witness, example, and encouragement to all. They are like our older brothers and sisters to whom we can turn for help in following Christ.

1. St. Augustine of Hippo

St. Augustine was born at Thagaste, in North Africa, in 354 of a Christian mother and a pagan father. He was a scholar and followed the pagan philosophers of his day. He lived with a woman without marrying her and had a son. Monica, his mother, never ceased praying for her son to receive the gift of faith, even following him to Rome. Finally, after she prayed for twenty years, Augustine went to Milan and there encountered the Christian teacher, Ambrose. His conversion began with that encounter and at the age of thirty-two he was baptized. He became a great teacher and writer of the Catholic faith. His best-known work, *Confessions of St. Augustine,* tells the story of his conversion. Two of his famous quotes are in this book. He became a priest and subsequently the Bishop of Hippo where he died, as the invading Vandals were closing in on his episcopal city.

2. St. John Chrysostom

St. John Chrysostom, born in 347 in Antioch, became a Christian in his early twenties after studying under a pagan preacher. Shortly after his baptism he became a hermit but had to return to the city because of ill health. He went on to become a priest, then Bishop, eventually, becoming Archbishop of Constantinople. He is considered by both the East and the West as one of the important Early Church Fathers. He is known for his preaching and public speaking, his denunciation of abuse of authority, his penitential life and the *Divine Liturgy of Saint John Chrysostom*, which is used in both the Orthodox and Byzantine Churches to this day. Chrysostom means "golden-mouthed" in Greek and denotes his celebrated eloquence. He was among the most prolific authors in the early Christian Church. Persecuted by both ecclesiastical rivals and the Empress because of his relentless preaching of the truth, he was banished and died in exile *in 407.*

"When you are before the altar where Christ reposes, you ought no longer to think that you are amongst men; but believe that there are troops of angels and archangels standing by you, and trembling with respect before the sovereign Master of Heaven and earth. Therefore, when you are in church, be there in silence, fear, and veneration."

3. St. Teresa of Lisieux

St. Therese was a Roman Catholic Carmelite nun who lived from 1873 to 1897. Having entered the convent of Lisieux at the age of fifteen, with special permission of the Holy Father, she quietly lived a life of holiness. She followed what she called "her Little Way" of complete trust and abandonment to Jesus and doing everything for love of Him. When she became ill with tuberculosis and was close to death, one of the sisters remarked "What will we be able to say about Sister Therese, she did nothing." Before dying at the <u>age of twenty-four,</u> in obedience to her superior, she wrote a simple account of her life and her Little Way. After her death, the manuscript was printed for the various convents and shared with people whom they knew. It spread like wildfire, and everyone wanted to read *The Story of a Soul.* Miracles began occurring through her intercession. She was named a Doctor of the Church for her doctrine of spiritual childhood and abandonment. She is one of the most popular saints of the Catholic Church.

"Everything is a grace, everything is the direct effect of our Father's love–difficulties, contradictions, humiliations, all the soul's miseries, her burdens, her needs–everything, because through them, she learns humility, realizes her weakness. Everything is a grace because everything is God's gift. Whatever

be the character of life or its unexpected events, to the heart that loves, all is well."
-from *The Story of a Soul*, Autobiography of Saint Therese of Lisieux

Young Saints

It is possible for the young to have a deep relationship with God, heroic courage, and a faith willing to die for Christ. God provides His grace to all.

4. Blessed Carlo Acutis

Carlo was born in 1991 in London and died in Milan in 2006 at <u>age 15</u> after suffering from leukemia. When he knew he was dying he said, "I will offer all the suffering I will have to suffer for the Lord, for the Pope, for the Church." From the time of his First Holy Communion, Carlo fell in love with Jesus in the Eucharist. He went to Mass and Holy Communion as often as he could, and it was because of him that his mother returned to her faith. A child of his time, he loved computer games but would limit his time in playing them, seeing how they could absorb you and keep you away from people. Instead, he began a website project of researching and creating a display of the *Eucharistic Miracles* around the world. He visited miracle sites to photograph them until he got ill. His project can be accessed on the computer and large printed displays of his research have traveled the world and are set up as a permanent exhibition. His mother said about him, "His immense generosity made him interested in everyone: the foreigners, the handicapped, children, beggars. To be close to Carlo was to be close to a fountain of fresh water... [he] understood the true value of life as a gift from God, as an effort, an answer to give to the Lord Jesus, day by day in simplicity. I should stress that he was a normal boy who was joyful, serene, sincere, and helpful and loved having company, he liked having friends."[82] He was declared Blessed on October 12, 2006.

5. Saint Maria Goretti

Maria was a young Catholic girl living in Nettuno, Italy, South of Rome. On <u>July 5, 1902</u>, at the <u>age of eleven</u> and alone in the house, a 20 yr. old neighbor sexually assaulted her. When she resisted his attacks saying, "No, no, Allessandro, it is a sin," he viciously stabbed her and left her to die. She was found still alive and taken to the hospital where she suffered from an infection brought on by the lacerations. She died the next day. Her last words were, "I forgive Alessandro Serenelli and I want him with me in heaven forever." While he was in prison for his crime, Maria appeared to him in a dream and forgave him, which led to his complete conversion. He lived a holy life and when released from prison, became a Franciscan lay brother. On June 24, 1950, both Maria's Mother and Allessandro where present, when the Church proclaimed her a saint and martyr for purity at a Mass in St. Peter's Square. St. Peter's Basilica could not hold the half million people attending the ceremony. Although she died for purity, her greatest virtue was an unyielding forgiveness of her attacker.

6. St. Tarcisius

Tarcisius was a <u>12 yr.-old</u> acolyte, an altar server to the Pope himself in Rome, during the persecution of Christians in the third century. When Christians were imprisoned, the Church in Rome prayed for them and when possible, provided them with the Eucharist, to strengthen them in their ordeals.

---

[82] Stevens, Rev. Clifford. *One Year Book of Saints*. Huntington, IN: Sunday Visitor Books. 1989.

At times it was not safe for a Priest or Deacon to go undetected, so Tarcisius would volunteer to carry the Blessed Sacrament to them, along with food to allay suspicion. On one occasion he was set upon by a group of young rowdies who wanted the food and whatever else he had. Tarcisius fought to safeguard the Eucharist, and as a result was beaten mercilessly by the boys and later died of his injuries. He is declared a martyr of the Church.

Not So Young Saints

There is something to be said about "long lives led in His Presence." Old age and the crosses that come with that, have a way of detaching us, refining us, and preparing us to let go of this world and ready us for the next. God's grace never stops calling.

7. St. Katherine Drexel

Born in 1858, as a young girl, Katherine traveled with her father, visiting the American Indian reservations in the West, and witnessing their extreme poverty which moved her to compassion. On a trip to Rome, she approached the Holy Father to ask if there were missionary sisters who could come and help. He said to her, "You go." Katherine left her life as an heiress to the Drexel fortune, (her father was a partner of J.P. Morgan) when she became a nun in 1889. She founded the Sisters of the Blessed Sacrament whose mission was adoration of the Blessed Sacrament and care for the Native American Indians and African Americans. Her sisters opened 145 missions, started forty-nine elementary schools, twelve secondary schools and Xavier University of New Orleans. She suffered a heart attack in 1935 but would live on until 1955 when she died at the age of ninety. She had had her bedroom situated in the convent so that she could see into the chapel to adore the Blessed Sacrament from her sickbed. She was declared a

Saint in the year 2000. I marvel at the wisdom of God calling an heiress who would have the money to establish these schools for the poor!

8. St. John the Apostle

The story of St. John the Beloved Apostle is well known. He was the youngest of the Apostles and Jesus showed him a greater tenderness. His response in love was to bravely stay by Jesus through His crucifixion and death. It was he and Peter that first witnessed the empty tomb and came to belief in the Resurrection. At the foot of the cross, he was privileged to be given the care of Jesus' Mother Mary and moved her to Ephesus when persecution broke out in Jerusalem. He wrote the fourth Gospel, in which He witnesses to Jesus Divinity and calls us to faith in each chapter. He wrote three letters in which he repeats the refrains, "God is Love" and "Love one another." He was the only Apostle who died a natural death at the age of <u>one hundred</u> while in exile on Patmos. There he had the visions that led him to author the last book of the Bible, Revelation. Steadfastness in faith and constancy in love is what pleases the Lord.

9. Venerable Bishop Fulton J. Sheen

Bishop Sheen died in <u>1979</u> after open heart surgery. During his life of <u>84 years</u>, he was priest, professor, orator, radio and television personality, but a man of deep prayer. He made a promise early in his priesthood to spend an hour in prayer before the Blessed Sacrament every day, besides offering daily Mass and praying the Liturgy of the Hours. He came to be well known and loved by millions of people in his 22 years for the radio program, *The Catholic Hour*, which he began in 1930. Later he would be seen and loved by millions from 1951 to 1957, as he hosted a TV series, *Life Is Worth Living.* This was followed in the 1960's by *The Bishop Fulton Sheen Show.* He was outspoken about the threat of Communism to the moral and spiritual life of nations. He called people to faith in God and prayer. He was instrumental in the conversion to Catholicism, of a top-ranking communist leader in the USA, Bella Dodd, from whom he learned about the plan of communism to infiltrate the Church. After his death, people began praying for him to intercede for them. He was declared Venerable by Pope Benedict XVI in 2012. In July 2019 Pope Francis ratified a miracle, which happened through the intercession of Bishop Sheen, making possible his future beatification. Millions are awaiting that occurrence, for they see him as a saintly Bishop dedicated to the Truth and the spreading of the Gospel of Jesus in a troubled world. In the days of radio and television, God called an orator to serve Him.

APPENDIX F

THE JESUS PRAYER

SINCE APOSTOLIC TIMES, calling upon the Name of Jesus by saying, "Jesus have mercy on me," or "Jesus Mercy," or simply "Jesus," is common among Christians. In the Acts we read of Peter saying "I have neither silver nor gold, but what I have I give you. In the name of Jesus Christ of Nazareth, stand up and walk."(Acts 3:6) The phrase "The Jesus Prayer" specifically, refers to a traditional Christian practice of "ceaseless prayer" in the Eastern Churches, both Orthodox and Byzantine Catholic. It consists of repeating the short prayer, "Lord, Jesus Christ, Son of God, have mercy on me a sinner" or variations of that prayer.

This prayer sums up the Gospel: Jesus is the Son of God who became man and is the one we turn to for mercy when we realize our sinfulness. His purpose for coming into the world was to save us from sin and death and reveal to us the Father's Face of Mercy. The following two scripture passages contain an expression of this prayer. In the parable of the Pharisee and the Publican praying in the temple, the Publican's prayer is, "God, be merciful to me, a sinner."(Lk.18:13) In the Gospel story of Bartimeus, a blind man, he cries out "Son of David, have pity on me." (Mk.10:48) They both exemplify the soul's fundamental attitude before God, our Savior.

"The Jesus Prayer" or simply the Name of Jesus, is commonly prayed in two ways. 1. A prayer that accompanies us in the activities of daily life such as waiting in line, washing dishes, taking a walk. 2. A prayer practiced repeatedly through the day, even spending time praying it exclusively, to allow the prayer to enter more deeply into our heart. It is often prayed on a prayer rope of one hundred knots: a Russian Chotki or a Greek Komboskini.

The term "Jesus Prayer" in Eastern Churches refers not only to the Prayer, but also to a Method of Prayer and to a way of spirituality called Hesychasm or Prayer of the Heart. Hesychasm, means resting in God. In this practice of spirituality, the person strives to attain interior prayer of the heart in which the Jesus Prayer would arise spontaneously from within even while we are asleep. One surrenders to the action of the Spirit of God who enlightens, guides, and purifies our heart, to restore the Image of God in which we were created. In this way of spirituality under a spiritual director, the practice of breathing, in rhythm with 'the prayer,' is taught. The person experiences a deep healing from the tendencies to sin, and transformation of one's inner being over time. It is the way of prayer in monasteries of the East. [83]

In the novel, *Franny and Zooey* by J.D. Salinger, one of the characters is praying "The Jesus Prayer" and shares it with his friends. The very readable Russian spiritual classic, *The Way of the Pilgrim*, tells the story of a man trying to discover how to 'pray always.' He visits various monasteries and begins practicing "The Jesus Prayer" which helps him endure and respond to the events that happen on his journey. Recently, I found a video on YouTube where the Name of Jesus is sung a thousand times.

---

[83] Funk, O.S.B., Mary Margaret. *Tools Matter for Practicing the Spiritual Life.* New York: Continuum Press. 2001.

APPENDIX G

Absorbeat Prayer

By the Power of Your Love,
O Lord, Jesus Christ,
Fiery and as sweet as honey,
So absorb my heart,
As to withdraw it from all
That is under heaven.
Grant that I be ready,
To die for love of Your Love,
As You died for love of my love.
- Saint Francis of Assisi

ST. FRANCIS IS widely known and revered. The quotes below speak to his holiness. He founded the Franciscan Order and invited people to love and follow Christ more faithfully. From the beginning of his spiritual conversion, he was consumed by the realization of the 'poverty' of Jesus, who emptied Himself to become Man and emptied Himself even further, to die poor and alone on the cross for love of us. He was granted the stigmata, the grace of suffering like Christ, and bore in his body the wounds of Jesus in his hands, feet, and side until his death. St. Francis died at 44 years of age in 1226. His holiness was so evident, and the miracles attributed to his intercession so numerous, the Church declared him a Saint in 1228.

Taking his cue from the prayer above, St. Bonaventure, a follower and biographer of St. Francis, said in his biography of him, that St. Francis was " absorbed by Jesus. "

St. Thomas Cellano. one of the followers of St. Francis who lived with him said in his biography of him,

"...everyday his talk was of Jesus, how sweetly and tenderly he spoke, how kind and loving the things that he said to them. His words issued from a welling over of his heart, it was the bubbling forth of the spring of enlightened love that filled his inward being. Indeed, he was constantly with Jesus; he bore Jesus always in his heart, Jesus on his lips, Jesus in his ears, Jesus in his eyes, Jesus in his hands, Jesus in every other part of his being. How often when he sat down to eat, and thought of Jesus, or heard or spoke His Name, he would forget bodily food... What is more, very often while he was walking along meditating on Jesus, or singing of Him, he would forget where he was going and call upon all the elements to praise Him. And because of the wonderful love he bore and jealously guarded ' Christ Jesus and Him crucified ' in his heart, he was singled out to be marked in a most glorious way with the sign of Him whom in ecstasy of mind he contemplated..."

APPENDIX H

A BRIEF ACCOUNT OF THE APPARITIONS OF FATIMA

IN 1916, WHEN the world was embroiled in the tragic First World War, Fatima, a little village in Portugal was visited by heaven. On three occasions, three young children saw a vision of an Angel who taught them to pray and to make sacrifices for sinners, for 'God had designs on their souls.' With this preparation, a year later, on May 13, 1917, 10 yr.-old Lucia and her young cousins, 9 yr. old Francesco and 6 yr. old Jacinta saw an apparition of a "beautiful lady" who would later identify herself as Our Lady of the Rosary. In a series of six apparitions on the 13th of the month from May to Oct., she would reveal to them that war is a chastisement for sin, that if the world did not repent there would be another and more terrible war, that many sinners go to hell because there is no one to pray for them and she gave them a vision of hell to show its reality. She asked them to commit to praying, especially the rosary, and taught them special prayers to say when they suffered. She asked if they were willing to suffer for the salvations of sinners and the children willingly offered themselves. She wanted her messages shared with everyone.

After the first apparition the news spread, and crowds of people began arriving to be present when the apparitions occurred. Lucia's mother did not believe her at first and took her to the priest who told her it may be the devil deceiving her. Our Blessed Mother kept coming. The secular authorities tried to frighten the children by arresting them on August 13th (Our Lady visited them later, August 19th) threatening to boil them in oil if they did not share the secrets the Lady gave them or admit they were lying. The children were steadfast in their testimony and even prayed the rosary with the other prisoners in the cell. The authorities had to admit defeat.

Our Lady stated that God is greatly offended by the sins of humanity. Besides the next war, she predicted that Russia would spread its errors throughout the world and nations would be lost. She also said that Francesco and Jacinta would die very soon, but Lucia would live a long life to spread devotion to her Immaculate Heart (she died on Feb. 13, 2005, at the age of 97). To prove the authenticity of her revelations, Our Lady predicted a miracle would happen on October 13, 1917. Thousands gathered on that day in drenching rain, kneeling in the mud of the fields surrounding the apparition site. As the children experienced the apparition, those gathered saw strange phenomena occurring in the sky. The sun was spinning, varied colored rays were falling upon them and the sun began to fall toward them from the sky. People were terrified, calling out for mercy, confessing their sins, they could not move from their place so they fell to the ground. After a time, the sun receded and all was normal, except that the ground was dry, their clothes were clean and dry and both physical and spiritual healings had occurred! This was seen by secular journalists who had come to debunk the seers, by atheists who came to scoff, and it was even witnessed by people living up to forty miles away. The secular newspapers printed pictures and accounts of the Miracle of the Sun. *The Miracle of Our Lady of Fatima*, the first movie of these occurrences was made in 1952 and others have been made since.

The church authorities rigorously examined these events for years, before proclaiming that they were of supernatural origin and worthy of belief by the faithful. Fatima is now a pilgrimage site, and all three seers are buried there. When Jacinta's body was transferred to Fatima from Lisbon, where she had died, it was found to be incorrupt and both she and Francesco are the youngest children not martyrs, to have been declared saints of the Catholic Church, not because they saw our Lady, but because they responded to her call to pray and offer themselves for sinners. They both prayed and suffered with great love as young children and died in the Flu epidemic of 1919. Sister Lucia is now called Venerable because of her saintly life and the church awaits a sign from God to declare her Blessed and then Saint.

APPENDIX I

POEM BY TEOFIL (TEOFAN) DUMITRU

MY HUSBAND WROTE poetry but primarily in Romanian. This English poem he had published in 1974 in the UNREA, a Romanian Byzantine Church publication. I treasure it!

I Wish You Were Here

When peacefully the moonlight
Goes down into the sea,
My heart can only tell you,
How much I think of thee.

And when at night low footsteps,
Walk through the cottage door,
Your tender face I see it,
Still glowing as before.

On windy nights I hear you
Rap on my windowsill,
And hopefully, I listen,
When everything is still.

Wherever you are, I am
With you, and you are near,
Look! The stars are here tonight,
I wish you, too, were here.

APPENDIX J

LENT: CATHOLIC TRADITIONS

IN THE CATHOLIC Church Lent is a period of spiritual preparation for the celebration of the saving mysteries of Jesus' Passion, Death, and Resurrection. It is marked by three themes, prayer, fasting and almsgiving (donating to the poor). Everyone is called to Fast in some way, and it came to be called "giving up something for Lent." Besides the common fast for all adults (eating only one full meal a day and two smaller meals, with meat only once), people will make a sacrifice of cigarettes, alcohol, going to movies, dancing, candy, reading novels, and such. Adults and children got creative. It was meant to be a sacrifice of something to which we were attached in order to focus more on God. The money not spent on these activities became the alms to give to the poor.

In the area of prayer, besides Mass and the rosary, a common devotion during Lent is the practice of making the Stations or the Way of the Cross. In every Catholic Church there are on the walls fourteen depictions of the journey Jesus took to His death on the Cross. They could be small wall sculptures, paintings, or simple drawings. Sometimes retreat houses will have life-sized sculptures set up around a garden outside. These are sometimes referred to as Calvaries. The Way begins with Jesus being condemned to death and ends with His burial in the tomb. This tradition came from people's desire to visit the Holy Land and walk where He walked. Not everyone can make a pilgrimage to Israel and these Stations are a way in which we can walk with Jesus on His last steps in this life.

EPILOGUE

"But if in your fear you would seek only
love's peace and love's pleasure,
Then it is better for you that you cover
your nakedness and pass out of love's
threshing-floor,
Into the seasonless world where you
shall laugh, but not all of your laughter,
and weep, but not all of your tears."[84]

---

[84] Gibran, Kahlil. "On Love," *The Prophet, p.12.* New York: Alfred A. Knopf, Inc.1976.